NEXT GENERATION
ARCHITECTURE

CONTEMPORARY DIGITAL EXPERIMENTATION + THE RADICAL AVANT-GARDE

JOSEPH ROSA

with 230 illustrations

Thames & Hudson

First published in the United Kingdom in 2003 by
Thames & Hudson Ltd, 181A High Holborn, London WC1V 7QX

www.thamesandhudson.com

© 2003 Rizzoli International Publications
© 2003 Joseph Rosa

British Library Cataloguing-in-Publication Data
A catalogue record for this book is available from the British Library

ISBN 0-500-28452-0

Printed and bound in the USA

-DEDICATED TO MY SON, HUGO WOERNER ROSA
J.R.

TABLE OF CONTENTS

ARCHITECTURE OF ANOTHER KIND

MARK ROBBINS

In a 1955 article published in *Architectural Review* on the New Brutalism, Rayner Banham talks about the inherent relationship in architecture "between structure, function and form," a "commonplace" which is only transformed by work that is "apprehensible and memorable." He cites art critic Michel Tapie's concept of *Art Autre*–different art or art of another kind–and writes of the potential for an *Architecture Autre* which might displace an aesthetic standard in favor of work that is "a thing in itself . . . with all its overtones of human association"

In his agile selection of projects for *Next Generation Architecture*, Joseph Rosa reflects on impulses toward the Cartesian and the baroque, between the rectilinear–associated with the rationality of modern building and technologies of construction–and the seemingly more idiosyncratic curve. While a rectilinear field may signify an economy of means and a response to functional goals, the suggestive indeterminacy of boundaries associated with the baroque nevertheless is also visible in the shimmering refractive walls of the modern "box."

In the lineage of architectural history, claims for form and its meaning are not new. Radical forms and spatial exuberance have been equated in the past with radical social and political propositions. A casual survey of the past twenty years alone for the interchangeability of these claims between the historically legible and the more abstract, for example, raises the question of whether form can have a politics at all–an inherent meaning which might give it independent power–as if architecture were an entity with will and the ability to determine or disrupt other social constructions. Recalling Mies van der Rohe's statement "I do not oppose form . . . only *form* as a *goal*," form may be inescapable in this arena, but it is not the main event. Architectural form is the consequence of a more complete reading of uses, materials and means of production.

The work in this publication is an expansion of an earlier exhibition *Folds, Blobs, and Boxes: Architecture in the Digital Era* (held at the Heinz Architectural Center, Carnegie Museum of Art), which looked at the range of possibilities offered to architecture by digital technology. The work variously demonstrates computing technology as rendering, as a means of fabrication, and most evocatively as a way to rethink architecture at many scales–rather than merely transcribing more efficiently what is already familiar.

The projects included in this book span from gallery and retail installations to the house, from public institutions to infrastructure and urban plans. While not solely the work of young practices–a case of their alignment with newer means of production–the projects do reflect changes in architectural pedagogy and architectural software as well as an absorption of manufacturing and production technology from other fields, such as animation and aerospace. Rather than digital work yet again being displayed as a novelty (some of the work dates back nearly ten years, and the technology has been in use in some form commercially since the early 1980s) we see a maturing sense of what it can do in practice. In ever more nimble three-dimensional renderings, digital technology has launched what is now a generation of identifiable forms—some with a historical lineage, others quite unprecedented—as well as manufacturing techniques.

When the economic downturn of the 1970s caused a dearth of building, a group of architects engaged in theoretical propositions through unbuilt projects that were labeled "paper architecture." Some sought an "a-referential architecture," drawn only from the formal language of architecture: geometry, scale and space—like a high modernist art avant-garde, without prior material or spatial associations. (Hans Hollein's polemical writing in the early 1960s took this further, stating that architecture had no purpose and was responsible only to itself). Some of these architects went on to build after the economic slump, and many of the younger firms presented here are influenced by this earlier experimental and confrontational body of work.

Some of this current digital design is more immediately linked to the possibilities and difficulties of building. The derivation of the forms is often driven as much by concepts of physical production and construction as by theory. Digital means allow a direct translation of complex shapes with processes like rapid prototyping and digital milling. Other architects are more conscious of using the smoothness of the computer rendering for seamless presentations with the gloss of advertising imagery. These younger practices have an eye on multiple national markets and branding as a part of their explicit mission—perhaps the most radical insertion of the discipline into expanded arenas of profit making.

The introduction and elevation of the digital brings with it the sirens' call of a break with the past, a seductive possibility that is part of any newer wave. Banham, perhaps having already seen the new displaced by the other new, did not predicate his revolution on form but instead on the impact and affect of architecture. Turning again to Tapie is instructive. Writing in the early 1950s, he called for artists with "temperaments ready to break up everything, whose works were disturbing, stupefying, full of magic and violence to re-route the public... into a real future." The digital works collected in this volume can provide an architectural program for the future, full of other possibilities that are at once unfamiliar and resonant. The power of this difference lies in the way things could be rather than the way they appear.

FOLDS, BLOBS + BOXES, V.2.0

JOSEPH ROSA

Since the Baroque era of the seventeenth century, architects have been trying to cast off the Cartesian grid, with its traditional notions of beauty and proportion in architecture.[1] Today, the term baroque, "an irregular shape," or the style, defined as "complex forms characterized by grotesqueness, extravagance, or flamboyance," describes both Frederick J. Kiesler's Space House (1933) and Frank O. Gehry's Experience Music Project in Seattle, Washington (2000).

Throughout the twentieth century, designers and architects have broken the orthodox box of Modern architecture, established by the International Style, questioning its ideology and pushing the boundaries of what shapes could be built. From Kiesler in the early 1930s to John Lautner in the early 1970s, these individuals redefined beauty and scale through materials and building methods outside the standard building vocabulary. Their innovative use of aluminum and poured-in-place concrete allowed them to create more curvaceous and fluid shapes. Their designs can be viewed as aesthetic precedents for understanding the smooth, morphed forms achievable with digital technology.

Today's digitally educated designers continue to redefine architectural pedagogy and practice, producing forms that can be described as folds and blobs, as well as the new digital boxes. Software programs that can laser-cut components on milling machines with an unprecedented degree of precision have made these forms buildable and have rendered other forms of architectural production unnecessary.

The evolution of nonrectilinear forms as constructible shapes is best illustrated in the connection between twentieth-century predigital and digital blobs. While predigital blobbers such as Lautner and Kiesler played a marginal role in mainstream architectural education and practice, digital designers of computer-generated blobs are becoming the norm today. This evolution in architectural aesthetics and practice resonates in Herbert Muschamp's review of "The Triumph of the Baroque," an exhibition at the National Gallery of Art in Washington, D.C.: "The affinity between the Baroque age and our own goes deeper than the formal complexity common to both. . . . I have seen the monitor screens of today's design studios, and they should give pause to those who think that computer-generated, so-called blob architecture has no place in the old bricks-and-mortar world."[2]

PREDIGITAL BOX-BREAKERS

The potential and limitations of digital design technology can be understood within the context of earlier attempts to operate outside the box of Modern architecture. Kiesler was one of the most influential thinkers of the predigital era. His Space House (FIGURES 1 & 2), a full-

1. (left) **FREDERICK J. KIESLER**
Space House, 1933
Modernage Furniture Company, New York, New York

sized model home designed for Modernage Furniture Company in 1933, was exhibited in their New York showroom. The Space House was clad in a streamlined organic shell with rounded corners. The continuous shell assembly allowed for more fluid interior spaces, akin to Adolf Loos's theory of Raumplan.[3] More importantly, it was the first built example of Kiesler's theory of correalism and biotechnique.[4] However, Kiesler was ridiculed in architectural journals of the mid-1940s that favored the rectilinear "Functionalist" aesthetic of the International Style. In a 1949 article published in the *Partisan Review*, "Pseudo-Functionalism in Modern Architecture," he defended his views: "Form does not follow function. . . . [F]orm follows vision [and] vision follows reality."[5]

Unlike Kiesler, R. Buckminster Fuller positioned himself in the design field as more of an inventor and a pragmatist. Fuller's projects, from his first Dymaxion House in 1927 to his Wichita House in 1945, revealed his critical thinking and willingness to co-opt alternative production methods from the shipbuilding and aircraft industries. Fuller's design for the Dymaxion Car (FIGURE 3), modeled after ship hull construction and fabricated by a shipbuilding factory in Bridgeport, Connecticut, explored methods of framing and cladding unorthodox shapes. The car (FIGURE 4) was framed in ribs cut from plywood sheets and sheathed in aluminum, illustrating how an occupiable,

2. (top left) **FREDERICK J. KIESLER**
Space House, 1933
Modernage Furniture Company, New York, New York

3. (top right) **R. BUCKMINSTER FULLER**
Dymaxion car, interior, 1933

4. (above left) **R. BUCKMINSTER FULLER**
Dymaxion car, 1933

bloblike shape could be created.[6] The short-lived success and aerodynamic failure of his Dymaxion Car (1933) left an unfortunate and indelible mark on his career.[7]

Fuller's four-piece Prefabricated 5x5 Bathroom Unit (FIGURE 5), built by the Dodge Research Laboratory in 1936, anticipates the smooth contours and surfaces of today's digital designs. One of the pair of three-foot-tall metal shells is the tub, and the other is the water closet and sink; two upper shells of similar shape create the enclosure for the bathroom. The exterior of the unit remained unfinished. This bathroom unit could be inserted into an existing building or new construction.[8] Aesthetically, Fuller's prefabricated bathroom featured a seamless, molded look that mirrored its method of mass production, similar to the design of today's plane interiors and mold-injected Jacuzzi shapes.

HOMES TAKE SHAPE

It was not until the early 1940s that a habitable architectural shape—not a Modern box—was successfully constructed. The Defense Homes Corporation financed Wallace Neff's 1941 Bubble Houses (FIGURE 6), and ten dumbbell-plan houses were built in Falls Church, Virginia.[9] Neff used an inflatable technique that pumped air into a rubberized cotton balloon secured to circular concrete slabs. When inflated, the

balloon was sprayed with concrete; insulation and wire mesh were added; and a final coat of concrete was applied to complete the roof. After the concrete had set, the balloon was deflated, and windows and doors were installed. This provided a two-thousand-square-foot, two-bedroom house that could be occupied within forty-eight hours.

The general public did not view Neff's "colony" as a success. Reports surfaced that "observers considered it unfortunate that public funds were being spent on such unorthodox houses." When the houses finally opened in November, photographs were taken with Mrs. Douglas Fairbanks, Jr., at one house where she reportedly consulted on the decoration. In efforts to make these hemispherical houses more conventionally appealing, Neff installed double-hung windows with shutters.[10]

Kiesler's Endless House projects (FIGURE 7) were never built, but might have been realized by this same construction method. He developed numerous iterations of the house in sketch and model form throughout the 1950s.[11] In an interview in the November 1950 issue of *Architectural Forum*, Kiesler concisely described the twenty-five-foot-high and sixty-six-foot-long house:

The Endless House is through its formation and construction more economical with regards to materials, fuel consumption, space coordina-tion, management, and maintenance than post-and-lintel concepts. The interior spacing equals a one-family house consisting of five bedrooms, one studio, playroom, living area, kitchen, dining space, a study and library. . . . Adequate bathing facilities and storage space. The entrance is through a center stairway or from a ramp outside the house.[12]

Kiesler's drawings, published in *Architectural Forum*, were among his most tangible; defined areas illustrated an unfolding of contiguous spaces, much like the interior of some contemporary blobs. In 1958, the Museum of Modern Art in New York commissioned an Endless House for its garden. Unfortunately, after two years the drawings were still not buildable, and Kiesler died a few years later.[13]

By the 1950s, the journals that once ridiculed Kiesler and Fuller were reevaluating their non-Functionalist approach. Thomas H. Creighton, editor of *Progressive Architecture*, argued in January 1957 that the "New Sensualism" was maturing in architectural philosophy, posing an alternative to the "box architecture" of the International Style. He elaborated on the critical role of new materials and methodologies: "The technical justification is appealing; plastic materials, from reinforced concrete to sprayed-on substances, make plastic forms possible."[14] Two years later, Creighton further defined New Sensualism, denoting three categories: sensuous, sen-

7. (left) **FREDERICK J. KIESLER**
Endless House, 1959 (model)
Collection of Whitney Museum of American Art, New York, New York

sual, and sculptural concepts. The first two categories related to bio-morphic and expressionist aesthetics, but Creighton's explanation of sculptural concepts underscored the relationship between the Baroque and the designs of the predigital blob makers:

> Much of the later Renaissance work, certainly most of the Baroque, employed sculptural plasticity (interior as well as exterior) to such a degree that at least elements of many buildings are sculptural rather than architectural. . . . Sculptural architecture is less restrained as it uses the plastic materials of reinforced concrete, or plastics them-selves sprayed on an armature that can be warped and twisted at will. This is not the application of sculpture to architecture, but rather the handling of architecture qua sculpture.[15]

A prime example of this sculptural concept of architecture for Creighton was John M. Johansen's 1955 Spray Concrete House #2 (FIGURE 8).[16] The shell-like structure was framed with steel rods that were bent into shapes and then covered with steel mesh and sprayed with concrete, a method traditionally used to form in-ground swim-ming pools.[17] In his description of the house, Johansen reflected on the feelings meant to be evoked by the space:

As I came to understand how symbolic spaces such as a labyrinth or cave are deeply set in the human psyche, I tried to re-create those experiences in architecture. In Spray House Project #2, I imagined the experience of living in a flower, swathed in its delicate protective petals, allowing between glimpses of the outer world.[18]

Johansen went on to distinguish his Spray House from Kiesler's Endless House designs:

> The Spray House #2 was not proposed as an 'endless house,' like Frederick Kiesler's, but a series of separate, overlapping layers. In this layering of shells, there was a sequence of human passage from the truly outside space to partial penetration to the innermost spaces. . . . Certain "shells" or "petals" break apart to emit passage of light, only to have their structural responsibilities entrusted to other shells.[19]

Like the Endless House, the Spray House was never built, but it reflects a serious attempt to construct a nonrectilinear shape in sprayed concrete. The project also documents the influence of Kiesler and Fuller on a generation of younger architects who, like Johansen, had small practices but were interested in expanding their ideology.

8. (top left) **JOHN M. JOHANSEN,**
Spray Concrete House #2, 1955 (model)

9. (top right) **RICHARD HAMILTON AND MARVIN GOODY**
Monsanto House, 1957
Anaheim, California

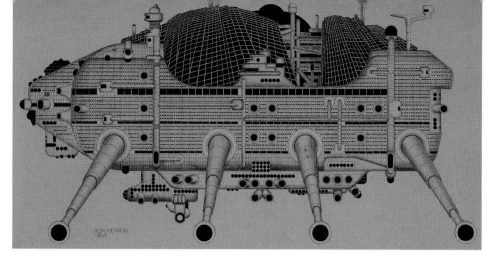

World War II technology spurred interest in new plastics and other materials as structural systems. This fascination reached its saturation point, however, with the unveiling of the Monsanto House (FIGURE 9) at Disneyland in Anaheim, California, in 1957. The Monsanto Chemical Company funded the research needed to construct the house, designed by Richard Hamilton and Marvin Goody. Monsanto wanted to produce a prototype house to demonstrate to the building trades the future of structural plastics in the domestic housing industry.[20]

The team developed a prefabricated structural module system that could be assembled at the site, bolted together, and painted. The finished house cantilevered out from its centrally located foundation, giving the impression of a floating dwelling with curved edges. Its exterior surface and curved edges were reminiscent of Kiesler's Space House, as well as Fuller's prefab 5x5 bathroom. When the house opened to the general public, it was furnished with designs by Charles Eames, George Nelson, and Eero Saarinen. Disney refurbished the house twice during its ten-year exhibition "to keep it a step ahead," but it was torn down in 1967 to make way for "Tomorrowland."[21]

Although well intentioned and conceived, the idea of structural plastics in residential construction was uncharted territory for banks issuing mortgages. Even Modern-styled houses with flat roofs were difficult to finance because bankers feared such designs catered to a

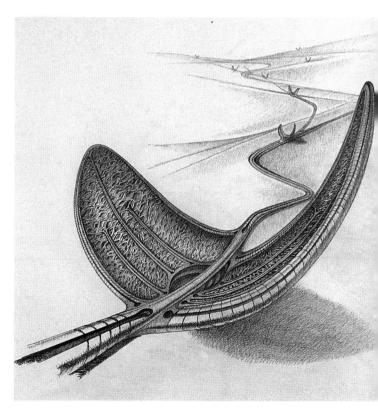

10. (top left) **RON HERRON (ARCHIGRAM)**
Walking City, 1964

11. (above) **CLAUDE PARENT**
Les Grandes Oreilles de la Lune (The Moon's Big Ears), 1967

small market and would not retain the resale value of more traditional pitched-roof homes.

REINTERPRETING TECHNOLOGY

After the war, the discourse of theory and practice in the architectural journals remained in flux. Many architectural critics and editors tried to pinpoint "the next step" in architecture, from articles by Siegfried Giedion, advocating a regional approach, to Creighton's further attempts to codify New Sensualism.[22]

The 1960 publication of Reyner Banham's seminal book *Theory and Design in the First Machine Age* spurred a significant shift in ideology. Throughout the 1960s, a variety of groups and small movements emerged, such as Archigram (FIGURE 10) in London, Metabolism in Japan, Superstudio in Italy, and the Inflatable Movement and Paul Virilio & Claude Parent (FIGURE 11) in Paris. Individually, these architects continued to question the notion of beauty, scale, and function, taking technology to a new interpretive level.[23]

During this period, one of the few architects to successfully build non-Cartesian, occupiable forms was John Lautner, whose Los Angeles poured-in-place concrete houses pushed the boundaries of function, technology, and tactility.[24] Throughout Lautner's career, the architectural press was ambivalent about his designs. Descriptions varied from "living stage sets" to "shapes [which are] unusual, inventive, fun, and exciting."[25]

Lautner's work was based on his concept of "disappearing space" and coincides with his use of concrete for residential projects. This construction method allowed for "compound-curve shells containing space without being enclosed or blocked and thus flowing towards the horizon."[26] Clear-span structures enclosed with frameless glass further emphasized the dynamics and fluidity of Lautner's spatial constructions. His evolution of forms culminated in the 1973 Arango House (FIGURE 12) in Acapulco, Mexico. Here, forms in plan and section are curvilinear and "bleed and leak" into each other in a lyrical fashion, thereby creating a continuum of space. Lautner's conception of "disappearing space" recalls Kiesler's description of the interior of his Endless House. Like Fuller and Kiesler, Lautner operated for decades on the fringe of mainstream modern architecture, exploring forms that defied traditional aesthetics of beauty and scale.

12. (right) **JOHN LAUTNER**
Arango House, 1973
Acapulco, Mexico

23

IGITAL DIMENSIONS

oday's digital architecture exists within this continuum. Architects orking in the digital realm who are changing the practice of architecure employ CAD/CAM systems, CNC milling systems, and such softare programs as Alias, Maya, and CATIA. While these tools were reated originally to produce airplanes, animation, and other conumer products—not architecture—they allow architects to generate igital typologies such as Folds, Blobs, and Boxes. Terms such as eauty, scale, and proportion, once used to describe the massing, rticulation, and texture of predigital vernacular, have given way to djectives like smooth, supple, and morphed, derived from digital-age ractices that are finding their niche in the ideology of twenty-first-entury architecture.[28] These digital typologies are the results of the lient's program, context, and site filtered through software programs. herefore, a digitally literate architect's work can evolve from box to lob and blob to fold. Yet this trajectory reflects the projects and comissions received more than the subjective aesthetic inclination of the rchitect to design within a digital typology. Simply put, these digital ypologies are the results of a methodology, not its starting point.

Any avant-garde movement becomes more mainstream as its aeshetic characteristics become codified and formalized into defining rincipals, but the digital typologies of Folds, Blobs, and Boxes have

distinct characteristics that render them unique. A digital fold in architecture can be an entire building (or two parallel facades) or an interior space that appears pleated like fabric or smooth with edgeless transitions between surfaces. A smooth fold creates a gentle transition and gives the appearance of a continuous surface that wraps a building or interior space. Airplane interiors are examples of smooth folds. While pleated or smooth folds can be digitally conceived and fabricated, with slight modifications in joining and finishing, folds can also be constructed with conventional building methods, such as wood- or steel-frame construction and poured-in-place concrete.

A digital box resembles a rectangle in its general massing. However, digital manipulation enhances the architect's ability to analyze and respond to the programmatic needs of a project and design a structure that becomes integral to the site. For example, the building can be bent and twisted to take advantages of views, reflect topographic conditions, or conform to prevailing wind patterns. The structure's overall massing may appear warped and its exterior and interior surfaces irregular. With respect to construction methods, a digital box is very similar to a digital fold. The digital blob, however, requires new techniques altogether.

Digital technology has made bloblike forms buildable while streamlining the design process from concept to fabrication. Using

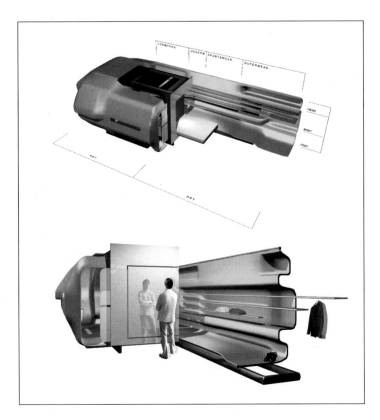

three-dimensional modeling software, architects can design the form and direct the cutting and production of building components. The supple, curved surfaces of bloblike forms can be precisely produced only through computerized cutting and milling of contoured, structural-framing members, and the overall form is an asymmetrical sculptural mass with no pure geometric qualities.

Needless to say, the aesthetic similarity between the predigital and software-based blobbers is undeniable. Predigital blobbers looked outside the standard building vocabulary toward new methodologies and attempted to adapt construction practices from other trades. The limited modes of production available, as well as the public's resistance to nontraditional shapes, nearly brought these explorations to a halt. The current influx of digital technology is expanding production capability and potential, opening once limited building trades. More important, today's consumer is more accepting of progressive shapes—from sneakers to watches—as designers are adapting new plastics, resins, and composite materials to everyday life.

These expanded modes of production visually link recent digital designs with predigital models—specifically the work of R. Buckminster Fuller. Joel Sanders's 2000 prototype Five-Minute Bathroom (FIGURE 14-16), commissioned by *Wallpaper* magazine, contains a bedroom, bathroom, and closet. To accommodate an "assem-

14-16. (top, above) **JOEL SANDERS**
Five-Minute Bathroom, 2000
Prototype

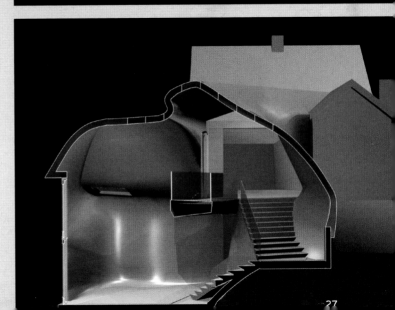

line" of functions from waking through dressing, Sanders
esigned the freestanding Five-Minute Bathroom with efficiency in
ind. In the morning, the bed can be retracted into the wall. The
nderside of the bed is a smart mirror—a programmable mirror sur-
ce that also functions as a screen to display time, weather, and
eight. The dressing closet, water closet, smart mirror, and bed
end together, creating seamless spaces that gently fold into one
nother. Made from prefabricated molded fiberglass, this unit is
esigned to be installed in existing or new construction. The folded
nd curved edges recall the molded contours of Fuller's predigital,
refabricated bathroom unit (1936).

Kolatan/MacDonald's addition to the 1997 Raybould House and
arden (FIGURE 17-19) in Fairfield County, Connecticut, is a bloblike shape
hat morphs between the existing house and its landscape. This two-
tory component creates free-flowing, seamless interior spaces. A
achine that reads digital files cuts the plywood ribs of the structural
amework. When assembled, the plywood is sprayed with a liquid
embrane that provides structural rigidity when dry. Whereas the
omputerized cutting and milling machines used to create these con-
urs represent technological innovations, the concept of plywood
orming a nonrectilinear, occupiable shape can be traced to the fram-
g of Fuller's Dymaxion Car of 1933.

7-19. (right) **KOLATAN/MACDONALD**
aybould House and Garden, 1997
airfield County, Connecticut

27

20. (above) **JAKOB + MACFARLANE**
Georges (restaurant), 2000
Paris, France

Georges, the restaurant at the Centre Pompidou in Paris (FIGURES
-22), France, designed by Jakob + MacFarlane, is an elegant solution
an interior space that pays homage to the past while looking ahead
the future (Jakob + MacFarlane won this commission in a limited
mpetition in 1997). Georges comprises four computer-generated,
uminum-clad blobs that rise up from the floor plane, also covered
th aluminum. To differentiate these shapes, the interiors are color
ded: red for the VIP lounge, lime green for bathrooms and coat
eck, yellow for the bar, and gray for the kitchen. The interior spaces
e also surfaced in rubber to dampen noise.

Three-dimensional computer modeling systems allowed the
chitects to generate and refine these shapes, which range in length
om twenty-six feet to sixty-eight feet. Digital production stream-
ed the process from design through fabrication. A boat-building
terprise on France's North Atlantic coast produced the structure.
omputer-directed water jets cut the aluminum structural framing.
e frames were then assembled, and aluminum panels were applied
hand.[29] Jakob + MacFarlane selected the boat factory because of
e hull-like shapes in their design—just as Fuller made his first
ymaxion Car at a boat factory.

Digital architects are referring to Fuller and Kiesler in their writ-
gs, as well. Reiser + Umemoto make a direct reference to Fuller's

21-22. (top left & right) **JAKOB + MACFARLANE**
Georges (restaurant), 2000
Paris, France

23. (above) **REISER + UMEMOTO**
West Side Convergence Project, 1999
New York, New York

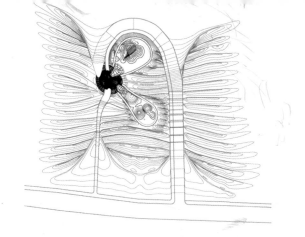

1950 proposal to construct a dome over Manhattan in their 1999 West Side Convergence Project (FIGURE 23)—while UN Studio (Ben Van Berkel & Caroline Bos) makes reference, in numerous essays, to Kiesler's Endless House and his ideology.[30]

The possibilities of digital production and design have allowed architects to restructure the post-World War II notion of mass-produced housing to create mass-customized housing. While numerous individuals are interested in this new frontier, Greg Lynn's Embryologic House© (FIGURES 24-25) is the most conceivable from ideology to materials. These highly adaptable structures can exist in a variety of climates and site conditions. Each bloblike house ranges from 1,800 to 3,200 square feet and sits in an earthberm that wraps the building's perimeter. Lynn explains:

> The [house has two floors and is designed as a flexible, curvilinear surface] and [is] composed of 2,048 panels, 9 steel frames, and 72 aluminum struts, networked together to form a monocoque shell. Panels, with their limits and tolerances of mutation, have been linked to fabrication techniques involving computer-controlled robotics processes. These include ball-hammered aluminum, high-pressure water-jet cutting, stereolithography resin prototyping through computer-controlled lasers, and three-axis CNC milling of wood-composite board.[31]

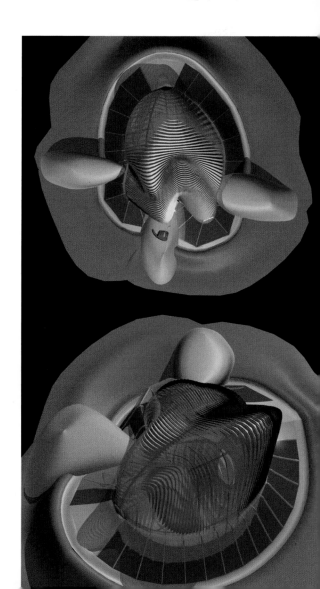

24-25. (right) **GREG LYNN/FORM**
Embryologic House©, 1999
Prototype

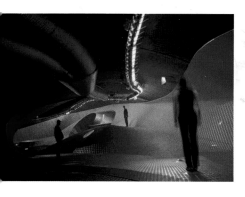

Prior to the advent of digital architecture, designers marginally explored blobs in the 1960s and 1970s, mostly for prefabricated use systems in Europe.[32] Very few occupiable predigital blobs exist, and few digitally produced blobs have been built. The first digitally based structure was NOX's (Lars Spuybroek and Kas Oosterhuis) 1997 Water Pavilion for Delta Expo "Waterland" in Zeeland, The Netherlands (FIGURES 26-27). The building is a wavy, elongated blob sheathed in stainless steel. The shape of the Water Pavilion is derived from fourteen ellipses that were digitally configured to establish the structure's overall massing. An interactive installation intended to educate the public about saltwater and freshwater systems is integral to the design. Activated by the movement of visitors through the space, seventeen sensors in the walls signal the filling and emptying of pools of water in the floor. The environment is thus in a constant state of metamorphosis.

Neil M. Denari's 1996 Interrupted Projections (FIGURE 28) is among the first built examples of an interior space created by folding. Gallery MA, located on the third floor of a six-story building in Tokyo, Japan, showcases exhibitions and installations of architecture and related design. The design juxtaposes flat end walls with smooth, folded side walls, giving the overall impression of a space defined by a curved enclosure. This three-month installation, commissioned by the gallery,

26-27. (top) **NOX**
Water Pavilion, 1997
Zeeland, The Netherlands

28. (above) **NEIL M. DENARI**
Interrupted Projections, 1996
Tokyo, Japan

was constructed as a second skin that bends and folds to form a contiguous surface unifying floor, ceiling, and walls.

Completed in 1999, the Korean Presbyterian Church (FIGURE 29) in Queens, New York, by Greg Lynn, Douglas Garofalo, and Michael McInturf, has been referred to as a bloblike structure. However, on closer examination, it seems more foldlike in massing and articulation.[33] The church was the first successful effort made possible by digital collaboration—each partner lived in a different state, and the building was conceived entirely in bits and bytes on the computer.

In fact, the terms fold or foldings were significant to architectural discourse and practice in the early 1990s, even prior to the digital fold in architecture. Moreover, the software programs that manipulate surfaces into non-Cartesian forms have precipitated further exploration of various critical theories, most notably Gilles Deleuze's notion of the fold:

> A fold is always folded within a fold, like a cavern in a cavern. Unfolding is thus not contrary of folding, but follows the fold up the flowing fold. It endlessly produces folds. It does not invent things; there are all kinds of folds—Greek, Roman, Romanesque, Gothic, and Classical—yet the Baroque trait twists and turns its folds, pushing them, fold over fold, one upon another." [34]

Peter D. Eisenman was the first to use Deleuze's concept of the fold in architecture—as a design narrative—for his 1991 Rebstock Project in Frankfurt, Germany. The term fold also appeared in *Unfolding Frankfurt* (Frankfurt: Ernst & Sohn, 1991), a small publication on the project with essays by Eisenman and John Rajchman. And it was the 1993 issue of *Architectural Design*, "Folding in Architecture," guest edited by Greg Lynn, with essays by Eisenman, Rajchman, Lynn, Deleuze, and Jeffrey Kipnis, that set the course for the fold in architecture.

Needless to say, Greg Lynn is at the forefront of the digital design revolution. The first use of the term blob—in digital architecture—was also by Lynn in his 1995 essay "Blobs," published in the *Journal of Philosophy and the Visual Arts*. Lynn describes the digital blob as follows:

> A class of topological geometric types for modeling complex aggregates that exhibits the qualities of multiplicity and singularity has recently been developed. The most interesting examples of these topological types are isomorphic polysurfaces or what [in] the special effects and animation industry are referred to as meta-clay, meta-ball, or blob models.[35]

The purest architectural blob is Frank O. Gehry's Experience Music Project (FIGURES 13, 30-32) in Seattle, Washington (2000), the only

29. (top) **GREG LYNN, DOUGLAS GAROFALO, AND MICHAEL MCINTURF**
Korean Presbytarian Church, 1999
Queens, New York

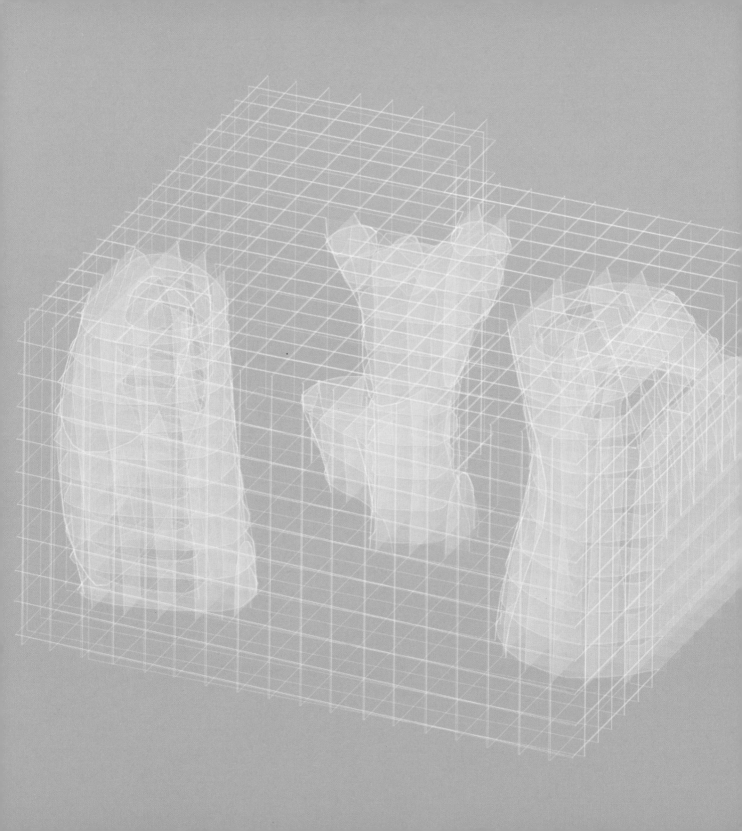

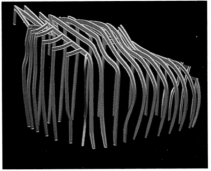 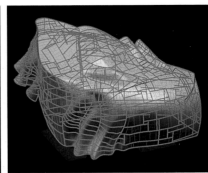

ilding to date conceived and produced with the aid of CATIA, a ree-dimensional computer modeling system originally developed for e aerospace industry. On a site adjacent to the city's iconic Space eedle, Gehry's Experience Music Project is an interactive rock music useum. The building contains six bloblike forms that recall the apes and colors of guitars once used by the legendary Jimi Hendrix. ehry first developed the design using physical models and then ade the transition to digital. From the undulating beams to the alu- inum skin that spans the color spectrum, Gehry's building illustrates at designs once only imaginable as fantasies are now buildable with gital technology. The technology allows architects to simultaneously sign and specify the project, eliminating costly and time-consuming op-drawing stages and reducing the margin of error in the produc- on process.[36] The building also marks a shift in Gehry's aesthetic way from the collaged articulation of shapes seen in his earlier build- gs, to the morphed and free-flowing surfaces made possible by ree-dimensional computer modeling. Gehry's EMP is a model for hat digital blob architecture can be in the twenty-first century.

Eisenman's 1997 Staten Island Institute of Arts and Sciences (FIG- RES 33-34) for Staten Island, New York, is a model for a digital fold. His terest in the fold (which spans the predigital and digital) has resulted numerous inventive ways of rethinking a critical architecture.

30-32. (top & above) **FRANK O. GEHRY**
Experience Music Project, 2000
Seattle, Washington

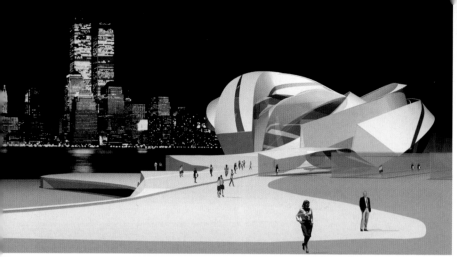

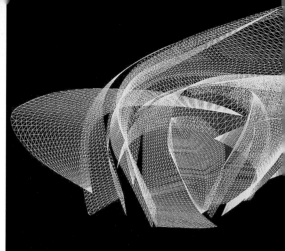

Designed to occupy a prominent site on Staten Island, with views of Manhattan, the building was to be part of a new ferry terminal and a point of arrival and departure for many commuters. Eisenman's studio used digital software to translate into his design the various pedestrian and vehicular patterns of movement through the building. Collectively, these paths of circulation generate a series of folded exterior forms and interior spaces that convey the idea of fluidity and motion.

Perhaps the greatest contribution of the digital blob and fold is its reshaping of barriers in normative architecture, allowing a new digitally morphed box to emerge. Bernard Tschumi's recently completed School of Architecture (FIGURE 35) is an excellent example of what the new digital box can be. Conceived to fit into an existing university campus environment, Tschumi's School of Architecture at Florida International University in Miami is a large complex of buildings totaling ninety thousand square feet. He proposes a courtyard flanked by two rectilinear buildings that house administrative and faculty offices, as well as studio spaces. Within this courtyard are two freestanding boxlike buildings—the yellow and red generators—where the lecture hall, reading room, gallery, and printing rooms are located. The overall plan responds to the movement of its future users, deflected wind patterns, and the buildings' functional programs. Tschumi developed the warped and irregular surfaces seen in the canted and twisted forms of the yel-

low and red generators using three-dimensional software. The result is a complex of buildings that will have a distinctive yet contextual presence in the overall setting of post-World War II Modern architecture.

In hindsight, Bernard Tschumi has played one of the most significant roles in furthering the dissemination of the digital design discourse by introducing it into the academic realm. In the fall semester o 1994, Columbia University's Graduate School of Architecture, Planning and Preservation, under the direction of Dean Tschumi, established the first "paperless design studios."[37] The introduction of digital design an production methods allowed students as well as faculty to rethink past methods of conceptualization and construction to generate new forms described by the adjectives smooth, supple, and morphed. By putting his school on the cutting edge, Tschumi raised Columbia's status as a forum for critical debates and educated a new generation of digitally li erate students. Today, many of the noted digital designers are either graduates of Columbia or taught at the school under Tschumi's tenure. Many architecture schools have since followed Tschumi's model of incorporating digital design into the core curriculum.

DIGITAL POSSIBILTIES

The advent of digital technology has also furthered the oeuvre of significant predigital avant-garde architects such as Zaha Hadid, Tom

33-34. (top) **PETER D. EISENMAN**
Staten Island Institute of Arts, 1997
Staten Island, New York

35. (right) **BERNARD TSCHUMI**
School of Architecture, Florida International University, 2002
Miami, Florida

Mayne, and Wolf Prix, rendering their visions buildable. Contrary to the general misconception that digital technology is a reductive force that will homogenize architecture, the buildings produced by digitally literate architects embody diverse ideologies and carry forward varying aesthetic explorations. Frontiers are widening as digital practices fuse with other mediums to generate new typologies. dECOi's invention, resolution, and implementation of Aegis Hypersurface (1999) illustrates one such typology. Aegis Hypersurface (FIGURE 36) was a competition design for the cantilevered "prow" of the Birmingham Hippodrome in England. It was proposed as a dynamically reconfigurable surface, capable of real-time responsiveness to events taking place in the theater. This digital dynamic architecture is a model for connecting interior or exterior building surfaces back to a core comprised of a "digital central nervous system" that would allow the surfaces to respond instinctively to the endless possibility of digital input, ranging from voice and sound to physical movement. Aegis Hypersurface is primarily a reconfigurable screen, where the computer calculation is deployed to a matrix of one thousand actuators that move what dECOi principal Mark Goulthorpe calls a "deep elastic surface." The possibility of sound-sensitive surfaces, or other data transposed into a dynamic environment with reactive characteristics, is an example of the optimistic, progressive thinking that would not be feasible without digital technology.

Exhilaration and optimism about what architecture can become is also seen in the edgy, progressive designs of Lindy Roy. Roy's design for the 2001 Wind River Lodge (FIGURE 37), an extreme ski experience facility in southern Alaska, employs sinuous surfaces that fold back onto themselves to create a twenty-six-room hotel reminiscent of a ski jump. A shape called "the helmet" houses the control tower and a bar with panoramic views of the peaks beyond. Lindy Roy's design methodology reduces projects to their fundamental characteristics and then reconstructs them through contextual/experiential, algorithmic-like systems to generate an experimental architecture. Roy's design for the Wind River Lodge is the ultimate example of an architectural embodiment of adrenaline. She pushes the envelope in ideology and program to create contextual digital architecture that becomes a metanarrative of site, program, and cultural underpinnings.[38]

The digital has also allowed architects to explore what could be called critical digital regionalism, in which the condition of the site, program, and cultural context are folded into the final design. IwamotoScott's 2001 Fog House (FIGURE 38) in Marin County, California is a good example of this new regionalism. During a portion of the year, fog, synonymous with San Francisco's Bay Area, passes over the knolled site. The path of the seasonal fog is incorporated into the con-

36. (top) **dECOi/MARK GOULTHORPE**
Aegis Hypersurface
Birmingham Hippodrome Foyer Art-Work Competition, 1999
Birmingham, England

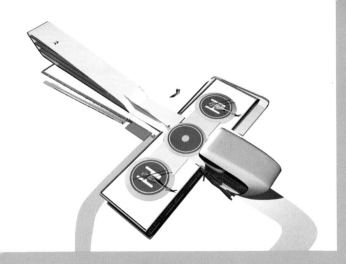

ot of the house, resulting in a void space that allows the fog to pass ough the house. Site-generated voids that reveal the fog as well as e view carve into the overall massing of this elegant, simple glass use. Another manifestation of digital regionalism can be seen in the dscape and urban design work of Field Operations (Stan Allen & mes Corner) and Tom Leader Studio.

Digital technology has influenced many areas ancillary to the oduction of architecture, among them the use of color, the setup of e architect's office, and the cultural context in which architecture critiqued. The digital realm is the real arena in which to study the taposition of hue, tone, and value to generate a color palette that n work in any context, from sun to shade. In Stamberg Aferiat's tsburgh Children's Museum invitational competition entry (FIGURE , the firm studied various color values of each surface in relation- p to one another to produce an effect that mimics the effect of ade and shadow. Colors were retooled on the computer to compen- te for the appearance of shade, which alters the hue. The satura- n of the color was adjusted to work in any light condition. The cooled colors were then matched from their digital files by a paint anufacturer.

Digital technology is also changing the makeup of the standard chitectural practice. Today, an office can exist in the space between the computer and the CNC milling machine producing the framework for the building. A template for the new office is foretold in the short-lived collaboration of Lynn, Garofalo, and Macinturf, with each partner living in a different city and no central location for the "office." The nomadic office (or studio) is ideal for the younger digital set, who teach at universities and institutes throughout the world. Conceptually, the office is the hard drive of the digital computer which houses all projects and can be accessed from any location. The only permanent address is e-mail. Examples of nomadic practices include the progressive studios of Ocean D and SERVO, both comprised of globally dispersed partners whose locations are subject to change in any given academic year.

The digital has also become a cultural context within which existing buildings and urban conditions are analyzed and critiqued. Martin + Baxi's Timeline: A Retro-Active Master Plan for Silicon Valley (FIGURE 40) is a highly theoretical work—a multi-part project that combines analysis and design in an overview of the recent past and the not-too-distant future. Baxi's primary objective is to rethink the city and architecture through a globalized digital lens. The project is a conceptual loop starting with Silicon Valley's architectural and urban logic, which is excavated and exacerbated, imported and recycled halfway across the globe to Bangalore, and then brought back to Silicon Valley.

37. (top left) **ROY**
Wind River Lodge, 2001
Chugach Mountain Range, Alaska

38. (top right) **IWAMOTOSCOTT**
Fog House, 2001
Marin County, California

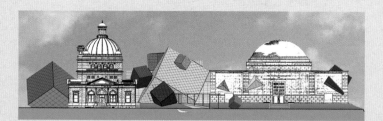

39. (left) **STAMBERG AFERIAT**
Pittsburgh Children's Museum, 2000
Pittsburgh, Pennsylvania

40. (right) **MARTIN + BAXI**
Timeline: A Retro-Active Master Plan for Silicon Valley, 2001
Silicon Valley, California

Martin + Baxi's critique of the urban sprawl and ubiquitous office building typology which typify much of Silicon Valley is analyzed and folded into a new methodology for rethinking office-park architecture and urban planning in the digital era. The final product is irreverent, playful, and—from an urban planning perspective—totally feasible. An example from this vast study is called "the Atrium Principle," which examines the abundance of office buildings with interior atriums. The study combines a range of variables—height, width, length, and size of atrium—into nineteen prototypical office blocks. The end result is a "timeline" of buildings encapsulating the range of sizes, from low "pancake" buildings to taller towers. More importantly, this methodology could easily be used as a conceptual model or filter from which existing architectural conditions could be reconceived through digital means to generate new aesthetic possibilities for architecture in the twenty-first century.

In many ways, the coming of age of digital literacy in the pedagogy, practice, and production of architecture parallels the evolution of architects like Frederick J. Kiesler and John Lautner from marginal to iconic status. Digital has also risen from the margins of the profession in a variety of different mediums. It first appeared in the early 1980s as the medium to produce computer-aided working drawings, better

known as CAD (computer aided drawings), then was adapted for rendering designs and enhancing aesthetic appearance for client presentations (the architectural equivalent of water color rendering mostly employed in the 1970s and 1980s). Finally, the medium's fullest potential so for has been as a tool in the conception and production of a new architecture.

Digital's maturity in the design realm has infused the pedagogy and practice of architecture with a sense of progressive optimism of what the future can be. Digital has become prevalent in all aspects of architectural production. As seen in the following pages of this book, the Next Generation of digitally literate architects have branched out beyond what one could only imagine a decade ago. In the quest to rethink normative twentieth-century Modern architecture, architects such as Frederick Kiesler, John Lautner, Peter Eisenman, Frank Gehry, and Bernard Tschumi have pushed the boundaries and laid the ground-work, making it ideologically possible for this Next Generation to build in the twenty-first century.

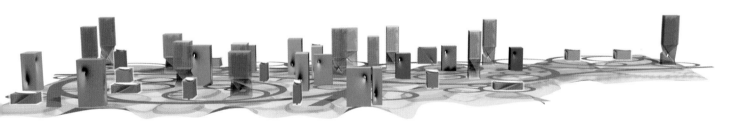

An earlier version of the essay appeared in the exhibition catalogue *Folds, Blobs, and Boxes: Architecture in the Digital Era* (Pennsylvania: The Heinz Architectural Center, Carnegie Museum of Art, 2001)

Henry A. Millon, ed., *The Triumph of the Baroque* (New York: Rizzoli, 2000).

Herbert Muschamp, "When Ideas Took Shape and Soared," *The New York Times* 26 May 2000, c. B, 32.

For more on the influence of Loos on Kiesler see Yehuda Safran, "In the Shadow of Bucephalus," in *Frederick Kiesler: 1890-1965*, ed. Yehuda Safran (London: Architectural Association London, 1989).

Frederick Kiesler, "Correalism and Biotechnique: A New Approach to Building Design," *Architectural Record* (September 1939): 60-75; William W. Braham, "Correalism and Equipoise: Observations on the Sustainable," *ARQ* 3 (1999): 57-63.

Frederick Kiesler, "Pseudo-Functionalism in Modern Architecture," *Partisan Review* (November 1949): 63.

Martin Pawley, *Buckminster Fuller* (Great Britain: Grafton, 1992), 62-63.

"[T]he first revolutionary dymaxion car was unveiled after only four months, on July 12, 1933. . . .Unfortunately within two months it was involved in a fatal accident that took place at the main gate of the 1933 Chicago World Exposition." Ibid.

Ibid., 89-93.

Alson Clark, *Wallace Neff: Architect of California's Golden Age*, ed. Wallace Neff Jr. (Santa Barbara: Capra Press, 1986).

——. "Building for Defense: Ballyhooed Balloon," *Architectural Forum* (December 1941): 421; "The Prefabricated Houses: Concrete Forerunner of the Movement," *Architectural*

Forum (February 1943): 67, 77-78

11. Frederick Kiesler, *Inside The Endless House; Art, People, and Architecture: A Journal* (New York: Simon and Schuster, 1964), 292, 308-10, 382-395, 412-5, 566-70; Dieter Bogner, "The Endless House," *Frederick Kiesler: 1890-1965* ed. Yehuda Safran (London: Architectural Association London, 1989), 42-55.

12. "The Endless House," *Architectural Forum* (November 1950): 63.

13. Bogner, 42.

14. Thomas H. Creighton, "Prologue," *Progressive Architecture* (January 1957).

15. Thomas H. Creighton, "The New Sensualism," *Progressive Architecture* (September 1959): 146. Also see Thomas H. Creighton, "The New Sensualism II," *Progressive Architecture* (October 1959): 180-187.

16. Thomas H. Creighton, "The New Sensualism," 146.

17. "Sculpting with Sprayed Concrete," *Architectural Forum* (October 1959): 166-68.

18. John M. Johansen, *A Life in the Continuum of Modern Architecture* (Milan: l'Arca Edizioni, 1995), 31.

19. Ibid.

20. "The Plastic House of the Future," *Industrial Design* (August 1957): 50-57; "Experimental House in Plastics," *Arts & Architecture* (November 1955): 20-21, 35.

21. Alan Hess, "Monsanto House of the Future," *Fine Homebuilding* (August-September 1986): 70-75

22. Sigfried Giedon, "The State of Contemporary Architecture," *Architectural Record* (January 1954): 132-137.

23. For a concise overview of this period and

participants, see Joan Ockman with Edward Eigen, *Architecture Culture 1943-1968: A Documentary Anthology* (New York: Rizzoli and Columbia Books of Architecture), 319-324, 365-368, 408-411, 437-441. For more of these individuals and movements see Peter Cook, ed., *Archigram* (New York: Princeton Architectural Press, 1999); Marc Dessauce, ed., *The Inflatable Moment: Pneumatics and Protest in '68* (New York: Princeton Architectural Press and The Architectural League of New York, 1999); Paul Virilio and Claude Parent, *Architecture Principe*, trans. George Collins (Los Angeles: Form Zero Editions, 1997).

24. Frank Escher, ed., *John Lautner, Architect* (London: Artemis, 1994); Alan Hess, *The Architecture of John Lautner* (New York: Rizzoli, 1999).

25. Joseph Rosa, "Independence and Dissent: The Domestic Dwellings of John Lautner," *John Lautner Architekt Los Angeles* (Vienna: Academy of Applied Arts, 1991). "John Lautner's Houses Take All of Hollywood as a Stage," *House and Home* (February 1952): 9; David Gebhard and Susan King, "A View by Susan King," *A View of California Architecture: 1950-1976* (San Francisco: MOMA, 1977), 7.

26. Dominique Lyon, "John Lautner: An American Dream," *l'Architecture d'Aujourd' hui* (April 1987): 93.

27. Reyner Banham, *Theory and Design in the First Machine Age* (Cambridge: The MIT Press, 1960), 327.

28. For an overview of software programs and theoretical ideologies see Alicia Imperiale, *New Flatness: Surface Tension in Digital Architecture* (Basel: Birkhauser, 2000). Also see Annette Le Cuyer, "Designs on the Computer," *The Architectural Review* (January 1995).

29. Claire Downey, "Georges, Paris," *Architectural Record* (September 2000): 128-137.

30. Jesse Reiser and Nanako Umemoto, "West

Side Convergence: Urban Process," *Architectural Design* (June 2000): 86. Unstudio (Ben van Berkel & Carol Bos), "A Capacity for Endlessness," *Quadernes 222* (1999): 62-67

31. Greg Lynn, "Embryologic Houses," *Architectural Design* (June 2000): 32.

32. For more on these monocoque structures see Gio Ponti, "Un Panarama di Alba, Di Risveglio, Di Inediti," *Domus* (June 1965) np. "Habitations Préfabriquées en Matieres Pastiques en France," *l'Architecture d'Aujourd'hui* (January 1965): 11; Leonardo Ricci: Village pouune communauté nouvelle, Riesi, Sicile," *l'Architecture d'Aujourd'hui* (June-July 1964): 86-88; "Blockwork: Andre Bloc's Habitat No. 3," *The Architecture Review* (October 1965): 236; "Laforma segue la funzione," *Domus* (March 1963): 14-15; "Prototype de chalet de montagne en bois collé," *l'Architecture d'Aujourd'hui* (June-July 1966): 64-65; "Pre-negozio Viaggiante," *Domus* (December 1967): 22-25.

33. Joseph Giovannini, "Computer Worship," *Architecture* (October 1999): 88-99.

34. Gilles Deleuze, *The Fold: Leibniz and the Baroque*, trans. Tom Conley (Minneapolis: The University of Minnesota Press, 1993; originally published *Le Pli: Leibniz et le Baroque*. Editions de Minuit, Paris 1988), 3.

35. Reprinted in Greg Lynn, *Folds, Bodies & Blobs: Collected Essays* (Paris: La Lettre Volee), 163.

36. Joseph Giovannini, "The Experience Music Project," *Architecture* (August 2000): 80-89.

37. Ned Cramer and Anne Guiney, "The Computer School," *Architecture* (September 2000): 94-107.

38. Joseph Rosa, "Algorithmic Foldings: The Architecture of Lindy Roy," *ROY/Design Series[1]* (San Francisco: SFMOMA, 2003).

RCHI-TECTONICS

NKA DUBBLEDAM

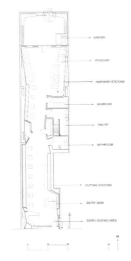

> AIDA HAIR SALON > NEW YORK, NEW YORK, 2000

cated on the Upper East Side of Manhattan, this 2000-square-foot commercial space is transformed by the insertion of a smooth and ulptural wrapper that Dubbledam refers to as a "smart wall system." This wall system is analogous to a motorcycle helmet. nceptually, the existing commercial space represents the hard shell of the helmet, and the foam inside is molded to the contours of the ad in Dubbledam's smart wall system. The helmet is a perfect metaphor for a hair salon. The void space between the helmet exterior d the molded interior—when transposed into the salon—becomes a continuous envelope that conceals the integral systems of lighting, ating and cooling, sound equipment, and floating mirrors, and that deploys into desks and seating elements creating an interior space folded surfaces that projects out and onto the exterior facade.

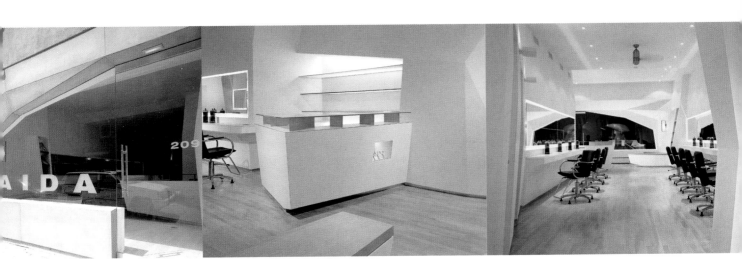

ARCHI-TECTONICS > GREENWICH STREET PROJECT > NEW YORK, NEW YORK, 200

This new eleven-story loft building and adjacent six-story warehouse renovation with an additional four-story penthouse will reinvig rate the once dilapidated urban condition of the lower west side of Manhattan with galleries, restaurants, and residential lofts. T building's structure is light steel frame with exposed concrete floors. The exterior walls are concrete with a folded glass curtainwall of the street facade.

The folded glass street facade of the new structure also wraps the new four-story penthouse on top of the existing warehous visually uniting the new and existing structures into one cohesive building type. At the ground floor, the glass facade folds out to for an entrance area for the residential lobby and retail and gallery spaces. The angled facade of the building is an innovative curtainwa solution, in which thin steel vertical extrusions connect to a suspended structure of insulated glass planes and horizontal aluminum fin This integral wall system was designed from conception to actual production on the computer and directly produced from the digit files. The folded sheets of glass were produced in Spain, and the aluminum fins that fit between these planes of glass were made Mexico. This innovative solution—made possible by digital technology—is one of the first built examples of folded glass employed on t exterior of a building.

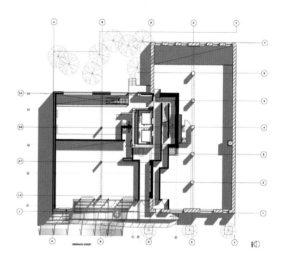

46 [ARCHI-TECTONICS]

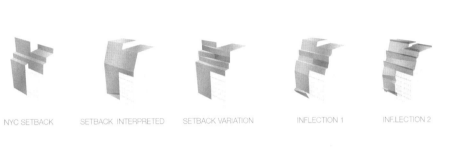

NYC SETBACK SETBACK INTERPRETED SETBACK VARIATION INFLECTION 1 INF.LECTION 2

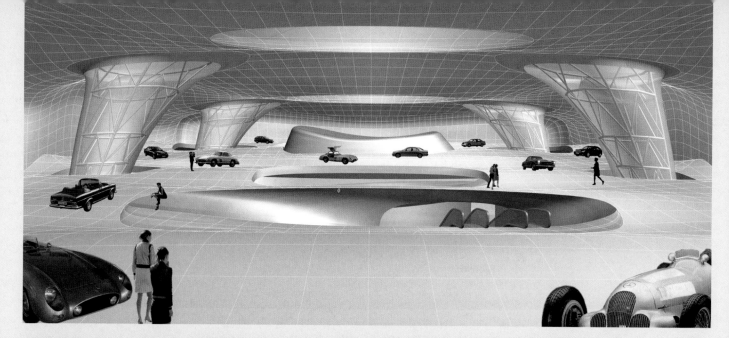

ASYMPTOTE

ANI RASHID & LISE ANNE COUTURE

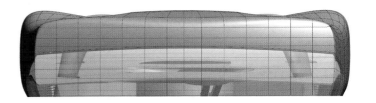

> MERCEDES-BENZ MUSEUM OF THE AUTOMOBILE > STUTTGART, GERMANY, 2001

This competition entry was designed to showcase the impressive collection of automobiles and related matter pertaining to the legacy of Mercedes-Benz. Asymptote design merges the overall building's structure with its architectural form, creating a monocoque structure reminiscent of the building forms generated by Frederick Kiesler for his unbuilt Endless Houses in the 1950s. Asymptote's bloblike building solution, fronted by a plaza, is clad in a combination of transparent, louvered, and opaque surfaces. The overall form of the building is wrapped in an aluminum-louvered skin. Glass wraps the main facade to provide visibility to programs such as the restaurant and museum shop.

To achieve this overall form and design concept, Asymptote combined the use of large-span structural framing—which provides for vast open spaces—with a topologically complex floor and roof surface to create roof and interior landscapes that are conceptually fluid and functionally flexible. Intersecting wave geometries cross the inclined roof and floor planes that span the entire width of the museum's hall, resulting in a vast, complex building form with an interior floor plane of various inclined and curved surfaces to showcase the museum's large automotive collection.

ASYMPTOTE > HYDRAPIER > HAARLEMMERMEER, NETHERLANDS, 200

The HydraPier is a municipal pavilion celebrating the city of Haarlemmermeer as a vital and new urban center. Adjacent to Amsterdam and the Schipol airport, Haarlemmermeer is comprised of an endless stream of airplane traffic and highway commuters. The HydraPier is situated within this highly active area and sited within an idyllic, artificially constructed pastoral landscape and shoreline that buffers the active city. Asymptote's scheme was the winning proposal from an international competition intended to showcase the city and Holland's tenuous relationship with the surrounding sea.

The HydraPier is a powerful architectural form on the shore of the Haarlemmermeer Bos, with an entrance bridge intersected by two cascading water-walls. The pavilion's architecture is comprised of two large spans clad in metal. On one side, the pavilion is deformed to incorporate an interior volume, while at the other end an inverse deformation in the canopy accommodates an exterior pool. The HydraPier also houses a multimedia exhibition space surrounded by a large deck that projects out into the lake.

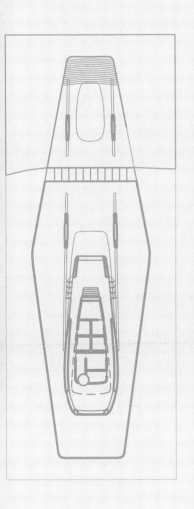

56 [PRESTON SCOTT COHEN]

PRESTON SCOTT COHEN › GOODMAN HOUSE › DUTCHESS COUNTY, NEW YORK, 2002

e Goodman House is 3,700 square feet and built around a nineteenth-century Dutch barn frame that will become the defining interior
ature. The timber frame was disassembled and transported from its original site near Albany, New York and reconstructed on this 160-
re hill site with views to the Catskill mountains. Cohen transposed it to its new site and inverted its condition, making the once hidden
nber frame visually exposed and the primary element in this well-lit interior. To stabilize the timber frame, a steel frame was introduced
rrounding the perimeter of the barn.   In order to intensify this inversion, the Goodman House turns outside in: the interior and exterior
e two mutually exclusive, interlocked spaces. The outer surface of the new gabled volume extends into a hollow core that traverses the
dth of the house. On the exterior, this core is a wind chamber. From inside the house, it appears to be a large habitable "beam" that
sses through the home. This breezeway converts from a screened porch during the summer to a winter garden by means of slide-up
reen doors and roll-down glass doors.

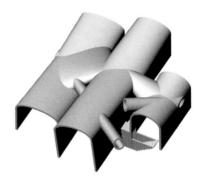

PRESTON SCOTT COHEN in collaboration with CAMERON WU > WU HOUSE > BURSON, CALIFORNIA, 2000

Situated on 185 acres, the Wu House is a modest 2,600 square feet. In plan, the house appears very simple in its overall massing, yet its cross-sections and ceiling planes are very complex forms. The house is a parallel series of three digitally morphed boxes. Each roof is formed from two elliptical vaults, joined end-to-end. At the junction, a cone-shaped vault passes crosswise through the longitudinal vaults and connects the three structures. In the interior, these intersections create lariat-shaped openings at the ceiling planes, resulting in spaces that flow into one another, creating a supple, smooth domestic box.

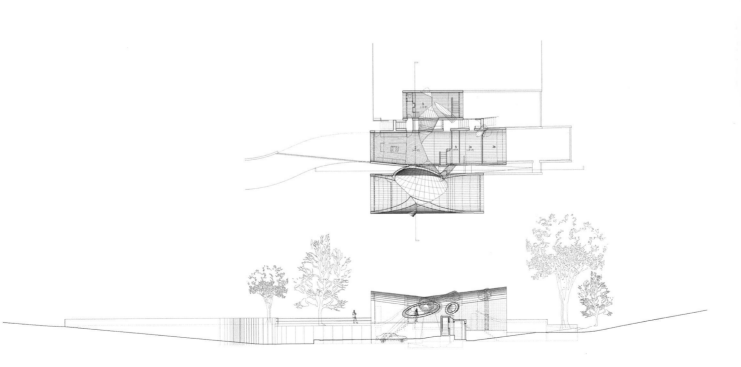

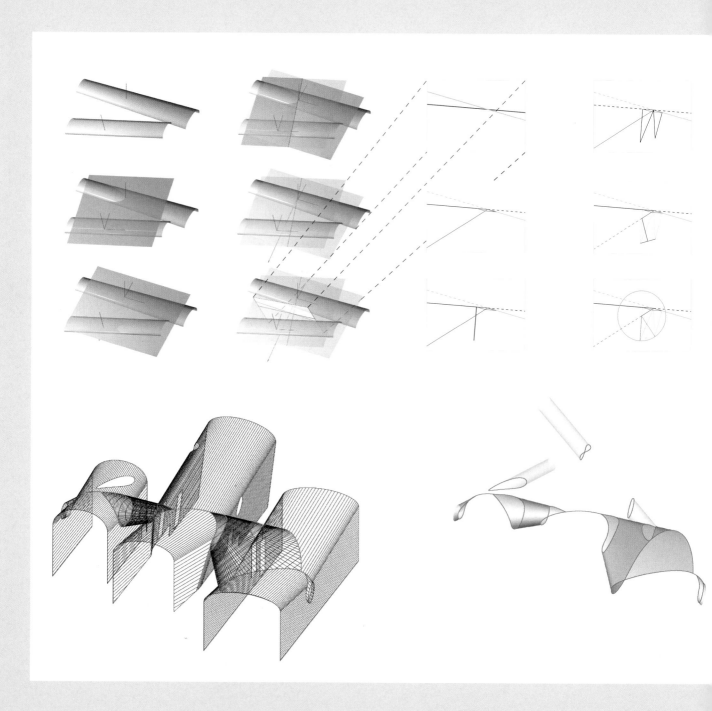

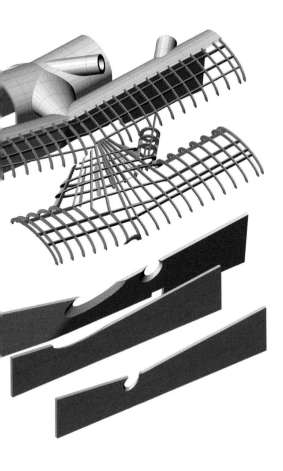

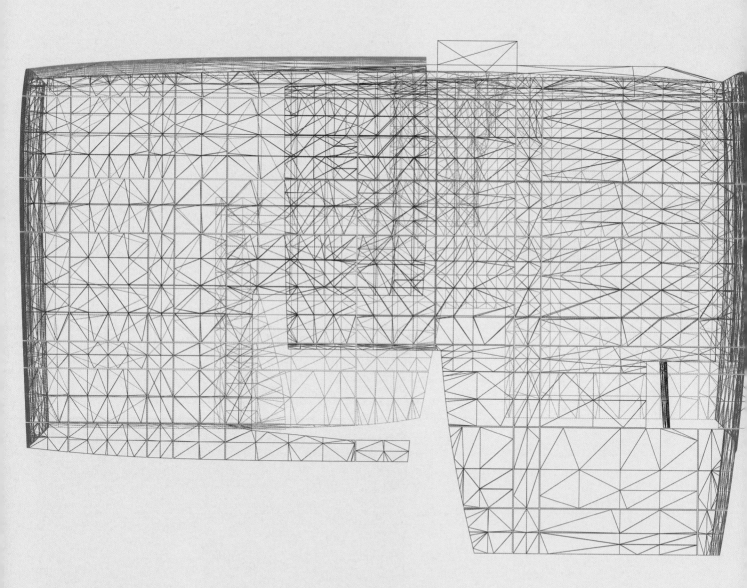

In collaboration with OBJECTILE > PALLAS HOUSE > BUKIT, MALAYSIA, 1997

ed on a densely wooded hillside in Kuala Lumpur, the Pallas House was designed for a young couple eager to explore new construction de possible by information technologies.

The configuration of the house is comprised of public and private spaces around a central atrium that is naturally ventilated. rmally, dECOi followed the local precedent of providing a shroud as a filter to the harsh tropical climate. This shroud is a complex, ved and perforated screen that wraps the volume of the house, spanning the roof plane as well. The perforated motifs added a "breath-" quality to the skin, opening to the east for morning light and protecting against afternoon sun from the west. While this skin appears be made of standard sizes, each one is unique and no two panel surfaces are the same. This elegant and delicate external skin was veloped and achieved by using Objectile software, which has been developed to directly link mathematically-generative three-dimen-nal modeling software.

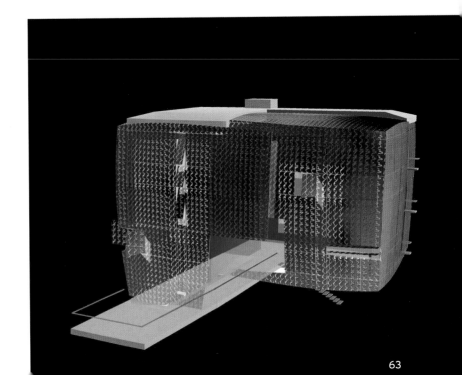

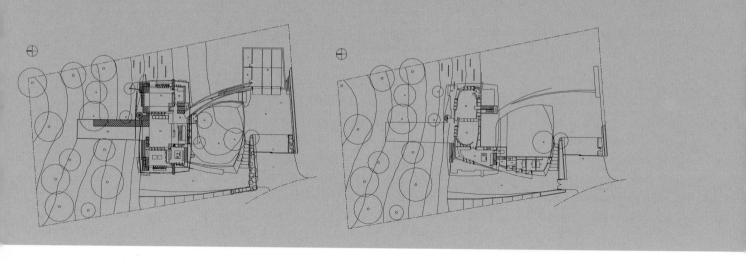

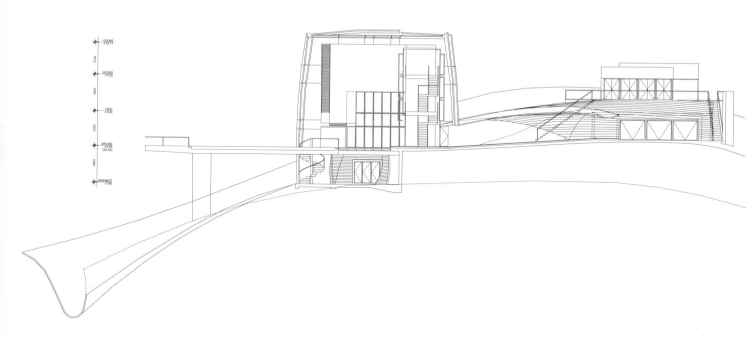

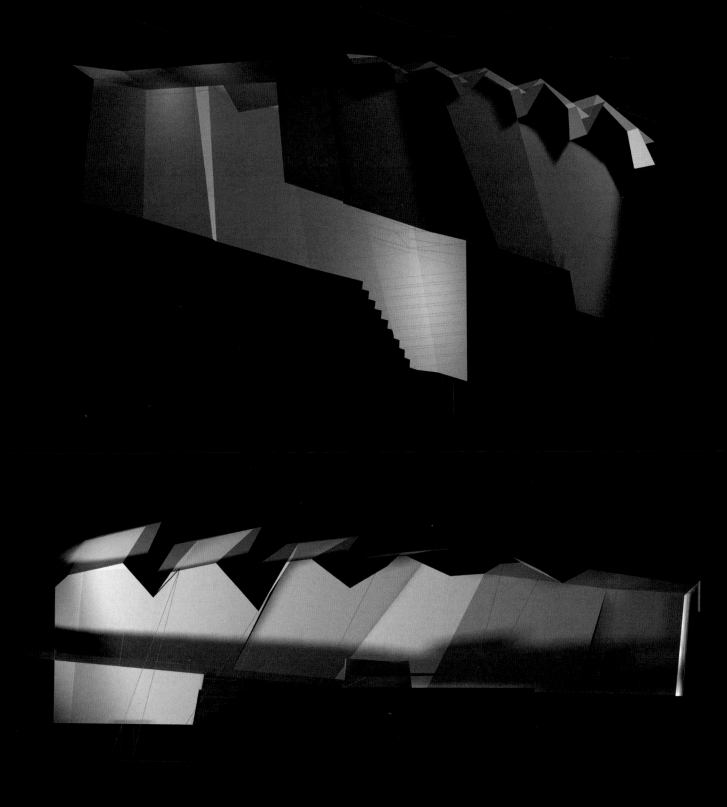

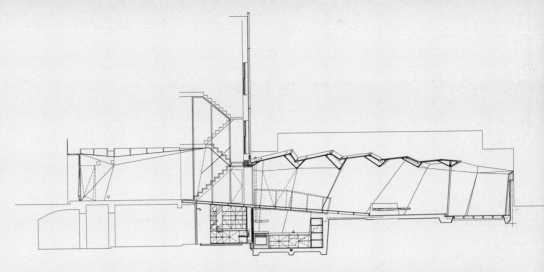

DECOI > DIETRICH HOUSE > LONDON, ENGLAND, 2000

This house, in an urban residential setting, was designed for a senior editor of an architectural book publishing company. The street facade appears restrained and in keeping with the overall context of neighboring townhouses. In section, however, the design reveals its true character with undulations in the vast, angular roof plane and interior wall surfaces.

dECOi conceived the house as fabricated primarily of aluminum framing, plasterboard, and multwall—a transparent plastic sheeting that allows light to penetrate and filter through the narrow structure. The form of the house shifts and morphs to produce an unconventional townhouse on a very restricted site.

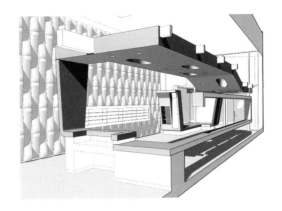

> L.A. EYEWORKS STORE > LOS ANGELES, CALIFORNIA, 2000-2002

cated on Beverly Boulevard, a prominent shopping strip in Los Angeles, Denari transformed a 1,150-square-foot retail space into a new atial identity for l.a. Eyeworks—one of the most progressive companies in the field.

Working within the basic parameters of store design, in which a sense of transparency from the street facade to the sales counter is andatory, Denari took this retail narrative and designed spaces and movements through a continuous suspended surface. This surface so performs and conceals numerous functions such as perforated ceiling plane (to absorb sound), window display, bench, shelving unit, d sales counter. By literally folding the functional needs with the formal conceptual aspirations of architecture, continuity, and eye- asses, Denari has produced an architectural resolution that has raised the bar in retail design. To mediate this interior space of seam- ss folded surfaces, Denari designed a series of mobile furnishings. The opulent retail space is completed by a wall of vacuum-formed nels designed by the artist Jim Isermann, filling an entire wall. The Isermann installation—a two-dimensional vertical surface with a petitive pattern on panels—becomes a graphic field juxtaposed with Denari's continuous suspended surfaces, resulting in a new identity r l.a. Eyeworks and a new model for retail design in the twenty-first century.

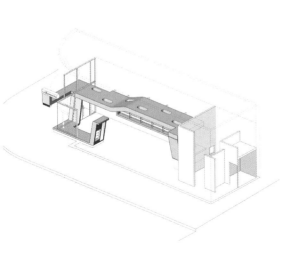

Designed for Tokyo, Japan, the Qualia Hotel illustrates a new model for the luxury hotel typology. The intention of the commission wa develop a concept for a high-end hotel for SONY Japan that would be an extension of their new sub-brands line of electronic devices. program for this new type has only one hundred rooms and delivers the ultimate in service and comfort for the high-end traveler.

Denari's design reflects the exclusive characteristics of the program, which are manifested in the formal configuration of the ar tecture. The rooms are disposed in a series of bays that transverse the block with private entrances allowing the hotel suites to bec visually disconnected from each other, hence providing a remote-retreat-like feeling. To achieve this, Denari produced a series of vert folded building forms that rise up from the base of the building and terminate in cantilevers that house the retreat-like suites. The res ing design is a visually dynamic new building type comprised of vertical extrusions that bend and fold, invigorating the notion of glc trotting in the digital era.

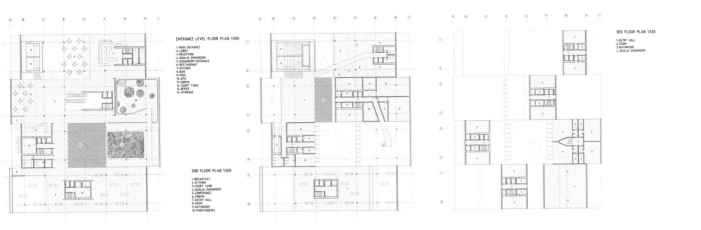

ENTRANCE LEVEL FLOOR PLAN 1:500

1-MAIN ENTRANCE
2-LOBBY
3-RECEPTION
4-QUALIA SHOWROOM
5-SHOWROOM ENTRANCE
6-RESTAURANT
7-KITCHEN
8-BAR
9-POOL
10-SPA
11-CINEMA
12-COURT YARD
13-OFFICE
14-STORAGE

2ND FLOOR PLAN 1:500

1-BREAKFAST
2-KITCHEN
3-COURT YARD
4-QUALIA SHOWROOM
5-CONFERENCE
6-CINEMA
7-ENTRY HALL
8-ROOM
9-BATHROOM
10-MAINTENENCE

3RD FLOOR PLAN 1:500

1-ENTRY HALL
2-ROOM
3-BATHROOM
4-QUALIA SHOWROOM

HOM FAULDERS

> MUTE ROOM > SAN FRANCISCO, CALIFORNIA, 2000

ute Room is a temporary installation of the Rooms for Listening exhibition at the Wattis Gallery of the California College of Arts and rafts in San Francisco. Visitors are invited into the gallery to recline on the undulating surface and listen to music. The undulating sur-ce that wraps the wall and floor is memory foam and acts as a sound baffle to enhance acoustical clarity in the existing rectangular allery. For Faulder, the employment of memory foam—an "intelligent" material experienced by many in the form of ear plugs used to ampen exposure to damaging sound decibels—also acts as a metaphor for listening. This is further emphasized by the color palette of eshy oranges and pinks that are reminiscent of the color tones used to illustrate the ear canal in Gray's Anatomy. The overall tactile sen-ibility of this digitally designed tranquil space becomes a metanarrative for movement, from the lounge-like foam surfaces that recede nd briefly record the trace of its occupants body to the registration of music to their ears.

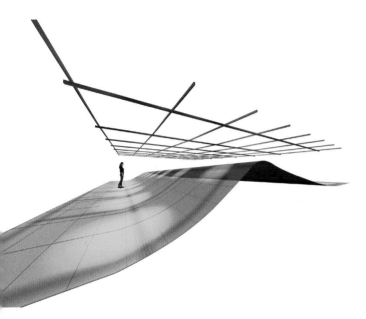

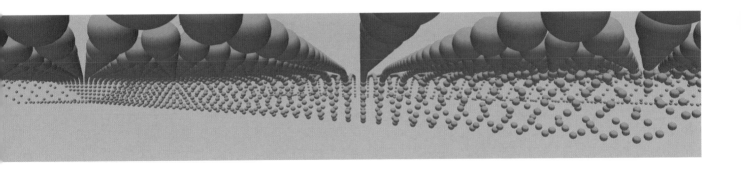

THOM FAULDERS > SUSPENDED FIELD > CINCINNATI, OHIO, 2000

[Fa]ulders' intervention for a parking lot in Cincinnati, Ohio questions the normative condition of a parking lot as a banal eyesore and trans-[po]ses it into a spatial diagram of movement and flow. Employing the standard parking lot vocabulary of curbs, signage, and pylons, [Fa]ulders created a suspended field that demarcates occupiable spaces—"plotting points"— for parked vehicles, pedestrian walkways, and [ve]hicle circulation zones. These plotting points demarcate corresponding height datums that are defined by lightweight orange balls sus-[pe]nded from cables spanning the entire parking area. From the outside of the parking lot these plotted points of orange balls collectively [cr]eate a visually warped plane that masks the function of the site.

Upon entering into the parking lot, the form-fitting surface visually dissipates, and automobiles navigate open spaces defined by [th]e suspended field. At the ends of the parking stalls markers hang down two feet from the pavement to function as "hanging curbs" that [ai]d in parking. Getting to and from parked automobiles, pedestrians circulate between the rows of stalls. Hence vehicles and pedestrians [ne]ver move through the same area. Slight winds will allow the suspended field to pulsate and undulate turning the banal condition of a [pa]rking lot into a kinetic design of dynamic movement that can only be conceived and produced digitally.

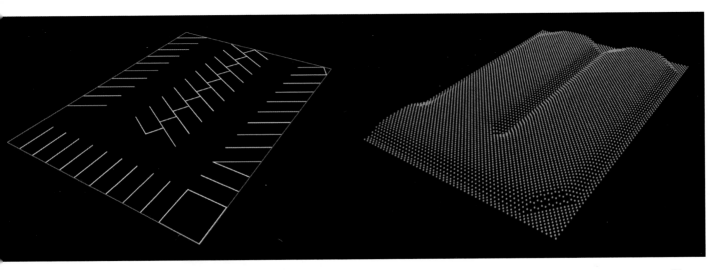

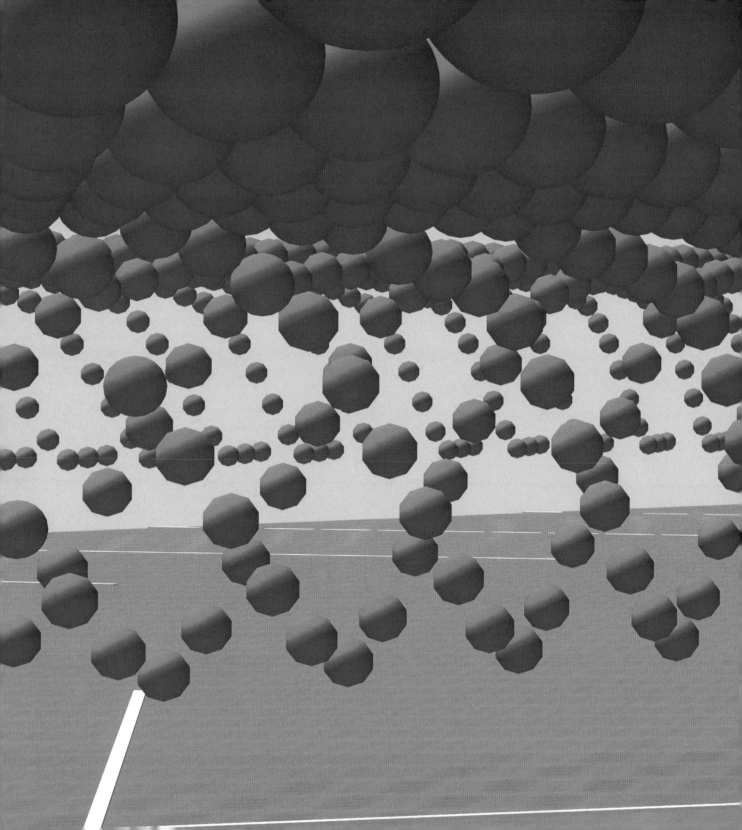

FIELD OPERATIONS

STAN ALLEN & JAMES CORNER

> LIFESCAPE - FRESH KILLS RESERVE > STATEN ISLAND, NEW YORK, 2001

"Lifescape" is the winning entry for the Fresh Kills Landfill to Landscape International Design Competition hosted by the City of New York in 2001. The 2,200-acre park project develops new and relevant strategies for a contemporary urban master plan. A major component of this winning scheme is a framework that allows for the development of a vast landscape for Fresh Kills that responds to local as well as regional factors—economic, ecological, and social. The framework allows for phasing development and interventions within this vast site to literally evolve over time in response to changing needs and conditions. When this project is completed, the site will have transformed from a mostly industrial, vast and vacant landfill into open spaces for recreational amenities and ecological reserves.

The Downsview Park Corporation was commissioned to oversee the conversion of a 460-acre military base into an urban park for the n
millennium. The objective of the PDP was to develop a fully specified design within five years that could accommodate changing scenar
in the future. Additionally, the park was to creatively integrate high-impact recreational programs with more passive dynamics of natu
ecosystems and wildlife.

To achieve the goals of the vast program, Field Operations—along with a team of consultants—produced a landscape framework co
prised of a matrix of interacting systems that is both integrative and flexible. The matrix consists of two diagrammatic systems. The fir
Circuits, gathers all the active recreation and circulation programs. The second, Through-flows, supports all of the hydrological and ec
logical dynamics of the site. Together, these constructed systems are the organs and lifelines that support and direct the unfolding nu
ber of future demands.

FIELD OPERATIONS > **NORTH DELAWARE RIVERFRONT PARK** > PHILADELPHIA, PENNSYLVANIA, 2001

ew Riverfront Park, planned along the Delaware River in Philadelphia, is designed to allow full public access to the river and associated n space amenities. The park, replete with a new river road, dedicated bicycle and pedestrian paths, smaller trails, fishing and boating ilities, and larger amenities such as restaurants, marinas, museums, market and event spaces, is conceived as a major public works ject that will establish a new "river" front door for future development and residents.

The new park connects the city back to the river figuratively and literally through a series of street extensions and riverbank toration techniques. The river's edge is developed as a diverse series of riverine and intertidal habitats interwoven by a new river lanade, which allows access while protecting the fragile riparian edge. Winging through the park, a new leisurely river road facilitates ess along the riverfront and provides new connections back into the city via cross streets. The road is also envisioned as highly igned and innovative elements using permeable surfacing technologies linked to vegetated swale and wetland systems for sustainable rm water drainage.

> BELGO RESTAURANT > LONDON, ENGLAND, 1999

e building was designed for an urban site tightly flanked by existing construction. The restaurant comprises an open-plan dining area
h adjacent bar/kitchen. In the absence of windows on the side walls, FOA stepped the curved ceiling plane with fixed windows that allow
ple natural light to fill the interior space.

The walls and ceiling are clad in horizontal wood siding to create a continuous surface, visually unifying the interior. In section, the
sign is bloblike and reminiscent of an oyster shell. Using digitally produced diagrams, FOA was able to explore the potential of various
ilding materials to achieve this shape.

FOREIGN OFFICE ARCHITECTS > YOKOHAMA PORT TERMINAL > YOKOHAMA, JAPAN, 1995-2002

uated between the Akarenga Park, Yamashita Park, and Yokohama Stadium, FOA's Yokohama International Port Terminal was the win-

g entry from an open competition for the project. Their proposal took the very normative condition of a pier and transposed it into an

gant metaphor for the relationship between water and architecture. The roof of this vast structure is a public park that allows this sea-

ally used pier to be active year round.

To achieve this built folded form, FOA employed ship-building techniques to produce massive building sections. From conception to

struction, the Yokohama International Port Terminal illustrates that invention coupled with digital technology and production can

ult in a new architecture and in one of the most important built examples to date.

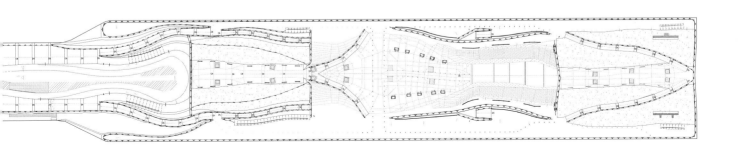

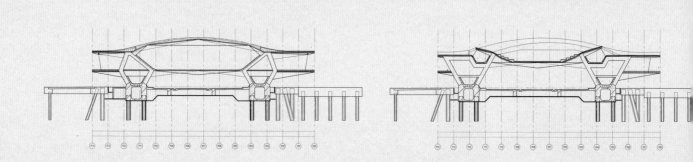

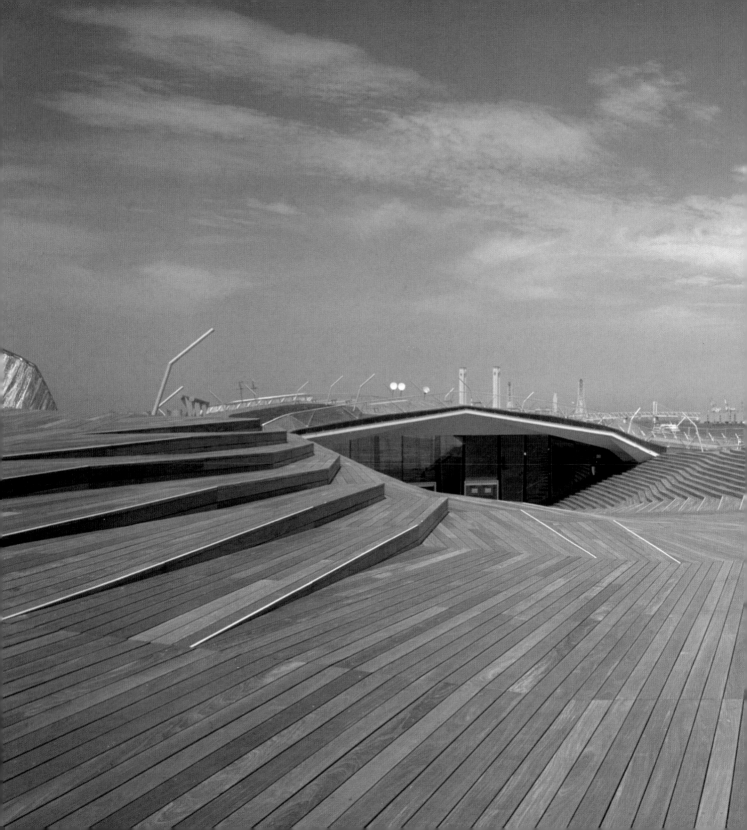

OUGLAS GAROFALO

> MANILOW RESIDENCE ADDITIONS > SPRING PRAIRIE, WISCONSIN, 2001-2003

is series of additions to a rambling former farmhouse sits on seventy-five acres sixty miles north of Chicago. The expansion to this rmhouse is meant to provide a comfortable retreat from the city for an extended family. The program called for various additions, which clude bedrooms, bathrooms, sunroom, screened-in room, lookout tower as well as a small animal barn. Garofalo's methodology for the sign ignored the quaintness of the existing typology—a red barn—and rather tried to reflect its acquired aesthetic properties in juxtapo-tion to the existing building vocabulary.

Digital production is evident in this building from the earliest schematic design through the construction process. The structural aming for these additions was created by Garofalo, then transferred via e-mail from the computer to a cabinetry shop for fabrication, here CNC, a computer numerically controlled router, cut all the plywood segments of the structural framing; these were later sandwiched gether and delivered to the site for assembly. At the site, the composite plywood framing was clad with three layers of plywood, and was en waterproofed with a plastic membrane. Over this a pattern of diamond scales made from titanium completes the exterior form.

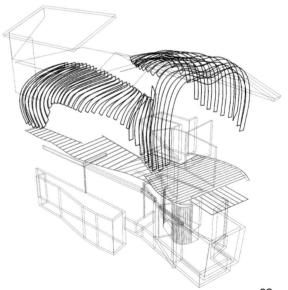

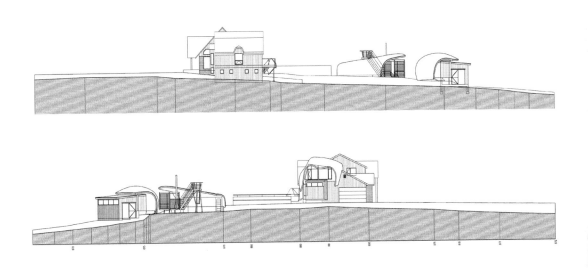

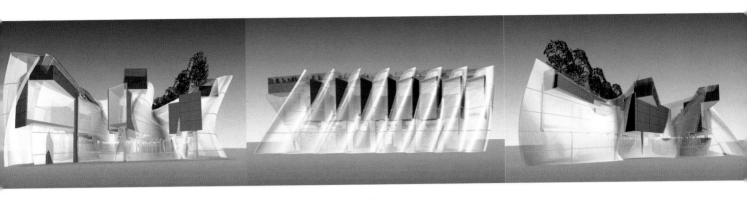

DOUGLAS GAROFALO in collaboration with RANDY KOBER > **LOESS HOUSING** > CHICAGO, ILLINOIS, 1999

Conceived for an urban setting, Garofalo's design for transitional housing can be adapted to fit a variety of urban sites. Reminiscent of a small walled-in city, the three-story housing system provides an elegant solution that limits pedestrian traffic, with spaces for living, working, and relaxing.

A slanted, sinuous, transparent folded surface gracefully wraps the building's perimeter to screen various functions: public space at the ground level, housing units at the second level, and terraced gardens at the third.

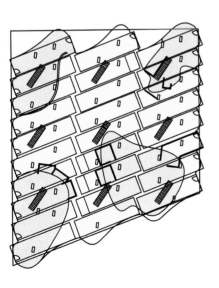 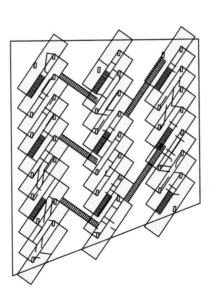 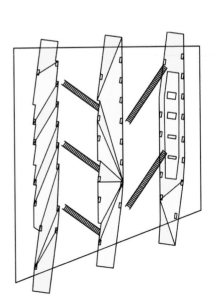

WAMOTOSCOTT

SA IWAMOTO & CRAIG SCOTT

Original volume of house   Void connecting primary views   Void creating fog access   Combined Voids

> FOG HOUSE > MARIN COUNTY, CALIFORNIA, 2001

Located on the ridge between the Marin Headlands and the San Francisco Bay, the site occupies a high point from which it has access to 270-degree views. Lisa Iwamoto and Craig Scott's design for the 3,500-square-foot Fog House seeks to engage the complex spatial and temporal dynamics of its site through formal and experiential activation of surface and landscape. While fog often blankets this region, making the site an island in the clouds, it dissipates within hours revealing the view. IwamotoScott took this aspect of the site as their narrative to directly and spatially engage these two conditions of view and fog.

In response to the client's desire to live in a single story of a glass skyscraper, they conceived the house as a single glass volume, out of which site-generated voids are carved. The house is organized around these voids—the Fog void and the View void—created through an extension of warped interior and exterior landscape surfaces. The living room and family room, which are bifurcated by this warped surface, are united by a terrace that allows the programs to function together. The two rooms, however, often become separated at times when low-visibility fog engulfs and splits the glass box's interior. As such, the fog makes rooms, and the spatial diagram transforms into that of a set of carved and discrete spaces. Conversely, on a clear day, the house acts like an open glass box with extended panoramic views.

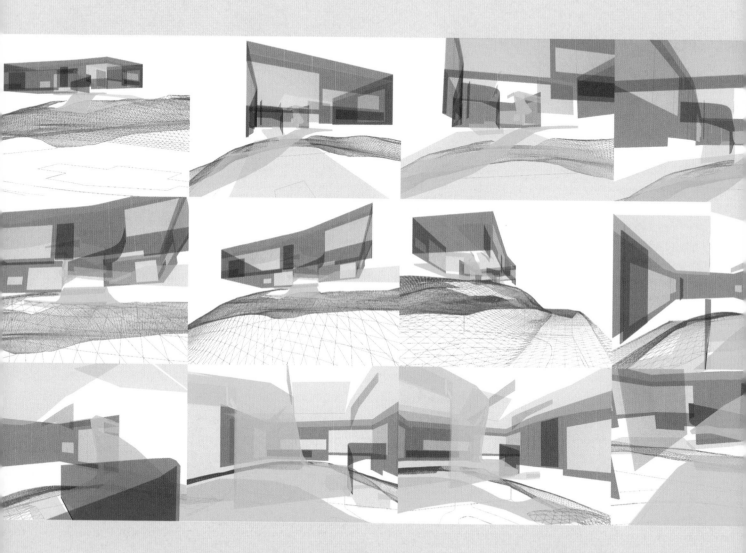

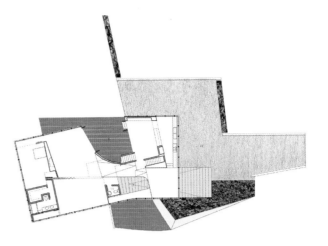

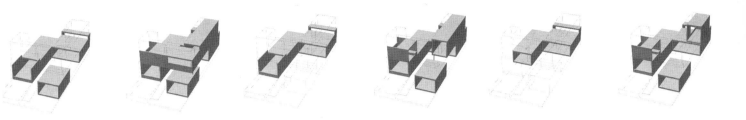

IWAMOTOSCOTT > LIVEWORKSHOPHOUSE > CLEVELAND, OHIO, 2002

he LiveWorkShopHouse was designed for the House: Case Study Cleveland competition held by the SPACES Gallery in Cleveland, Ohio.
vamotoScott's proposal is simultaneously prototypical, site-specific, and adaptable in nature. Instead of producing one resolution for the
te of fifty by one hundred feet (which is a variation on the typical lot of twenty-five by one hundred feet), they produced a strategy for
utable variation based on a three-dimensional scheme. Working with digital modeling they generated a re-configurable system of con-
tructable and spatial building blocks. The results were three permutations—THIN LiveWork House, MEDIUM Garden Guest House, and
/IDE LiveWorkShop House.

The 2,000-square-foot WIDE House, designed for a double lot serves as the base model. The house's configurational logic begins by
efining solid-void relationships among modular "building blocks" comprised of individual programs that meld together to create a new
rban resolution through digital manipulation. The design endeavors to develop a re-configurable prototype that goes beyond the current
anal view of modularity to reemploy and rethink in non-standard fashion.

JAKOB + MACFARLANE

DOMINIQUE JAKOB & BRENDAN MACFARLANE

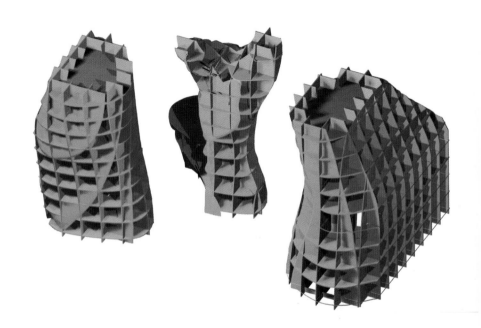

> FLORENCE LOEWY BOOKSTORE > PARIS, FRANCE, 2001

This project has been digitally conceived as a large rectangular grid of wood—defined by the average size of a book—completely filling the interior volume of a retail space. This gridded interior volume is then excavated to provide for needed occupiable space for circulation, selling, and storage for books that are not on the shelves. The results are three undulating gridded forms that act as stacks for books with concealed storage spaces within. Conceptually, the book is the fabricator of its own architectural character. The stacks appear as treelike forms, revealing the seriality of the grid that fabricated the space and modulating back to the scale and proportion of a tactile object held in the hand—in this case a book.

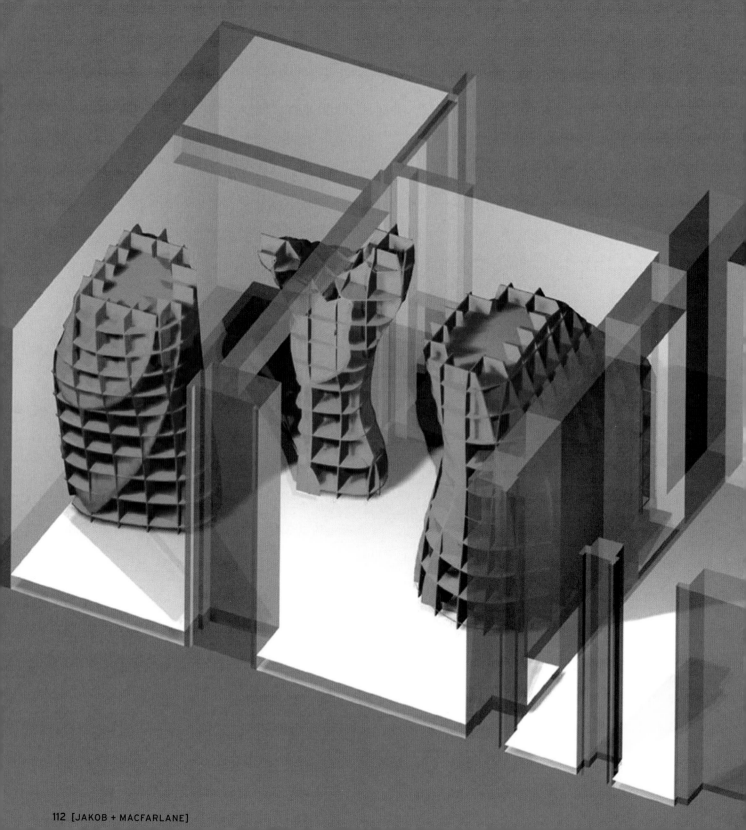

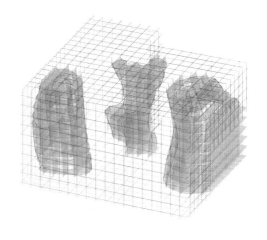

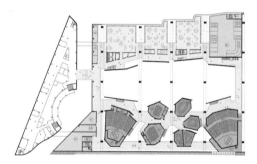

Jakob + Macfarlane's competition winning proposal for the Renault international Communication Centre illustrates why they are one the leading studios in France that are realizing digital architecture. Their design for the Centre—which will be completed in 2004—folds the various program requirements into one simple form. Within the overall massing of this simple building, with skylights that demarca the roof plane, are a series of shed-like forms that will house offices, exhibition spaces, restaurants, and auditoriums. These asymmet cally disposed, canted shed-like forms create public and private areas within the overall interior form, allowing for a vast centrally locat event space in the building's main hall.

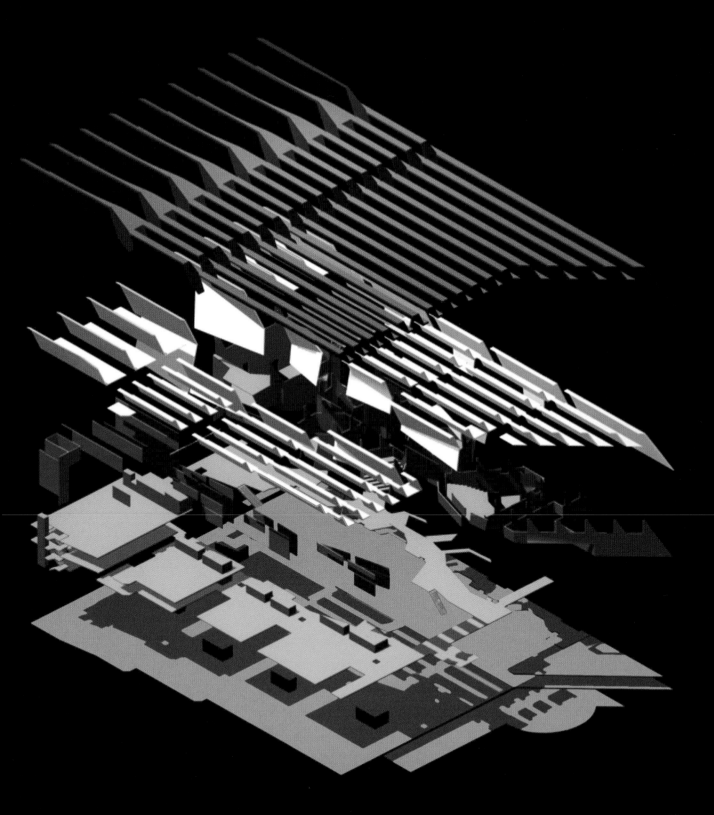

ONES, PARTNERS

:S JONES

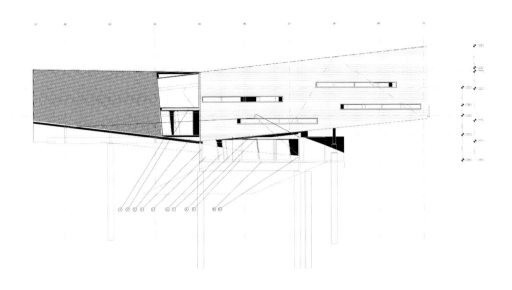

> ARIAS-TSANG HOUSE > BRISBANE, CALIFORNIA, 1999

Conceived for a steep suburban site bordering a dense forest of mature oaks, this 3,000-square-foot "machine" is well suited to the odern family. To screen views into houses on the adjoining lots, Jones placed large windows at the front and back of the structure and naller windows on the sides, similar to the location of windows in a loft space.

The house is a simple rectangle that twists and bends to reflect the topography of the site. These surface contours extend into the ving area, where both the hardwood floor and ceiling are sloped, further emphasizing the site's unique characteristics.

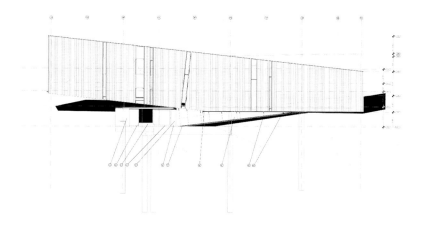

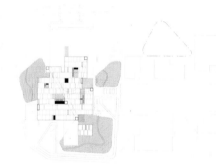

JONES, PARTNERS > **THE GRAND EGYPTIAN MUSEUM** > CAIRO, EGYPT, 200

Jones's entry for the open competition for the Grand Egyptian Museum plays with Leo Marx's *Machine in the Garden* ideolo transfigured through digital technology to the Egyptian landscape. The overall massing of the building is horizontally disposed and pe odically demarcated by towers and triangulated shapes that pierce the sand. The simple rectilinear character of this proposal inse itself into the arid landscape via an image like an aircraft carrier moving across the ocean. It is through digital three-dimensional mod ing of the existing topography and context that Jones's design becomes informed and reductive in its aesthetic, while furthering t notion of the Machine in the digital Garden for the twenty-first century.

> RESI-RISE SKYSCRAPER > NEW YORK, NEW YORK, 2000

posed for the Columbus Circle site in New York City, Sulan Kolatan and William MacDonald's visionary design merges current critical hitectural theory with skyscraper typology to formulate a completely new digital way to generate a vertical city in the twenty-first tury.

Kolatan/MacDonald create a "vertical urbanism" with their design. The Resi-Rise Skyscraper was conceived as a series of vertical ding "lots," each with its own maximum allowable zoning envelope. When these "lots" or floor plates are stacked, they produce a verti-building comprised of zoning envelopes to create a dynamic shape that registers views and adjacencies of existing buildings by defor-tions of the zoning envelopes. Collectively, the building is a structural frame with plug-in "pods." Working with the notion of mass tomization, each pod is customized for each tenant and can be modified per new leases. The architects continually play a role in the difications to these pods and work for the owner in producing these modifications or "new models" for the new tenants.

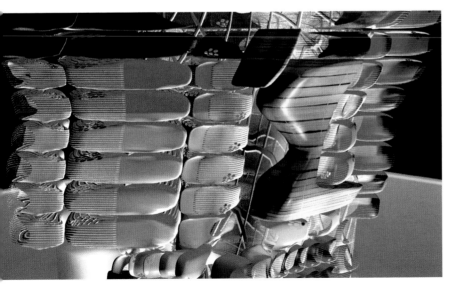
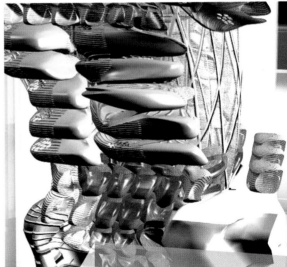

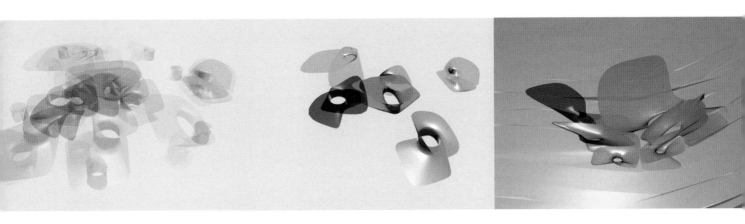

KOLATAN / MACDONALD > META-HOM > CHARLOTTESVILLE, VIRGINIA, 2001-

signed for a two hundred-acre site of rolling hills near Charlottesville, Virginia, the program called for an 8,000-square-foot main house th two small guest homes. The property is a subdivision of an adjacent five hundred-acre estate that has an historic main house signed by Thomas Jefferson. The clients presently own this vast estate, live in the Jeffersonian home, and also own an apartment in w York City designed by Kolatan/MacDonald.

Theoretically, the Meta-HOM project is a house launched from the parts and particularities of a domestic program. It investigates construction of "House & Home" as a distributed dynamic system. Attributes, relationships, and hierarchies of this dynamic system provided by a number of co-citation maps charted for the house and evolved throughout the design process. Co-citation maps consist thematically or categorically organized clusters with cross-thematic or cross-categorical connections where co-citation occurs. The sign strategy uses information from both these maps to construct hollow columnar topologies housed with autonomous program clus- s. This methodology also informs an aesthetic that displaces structure for program. Hence the monocoque structure of the Meta-HOM comes self-supporting. These cylindrical topologies encode a number of structurally self-sufficient micro-HOMzones. Multiple micro- Mzones thus have their own programmatic and morphological identity.

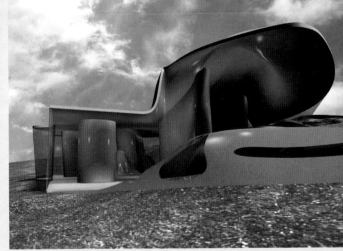

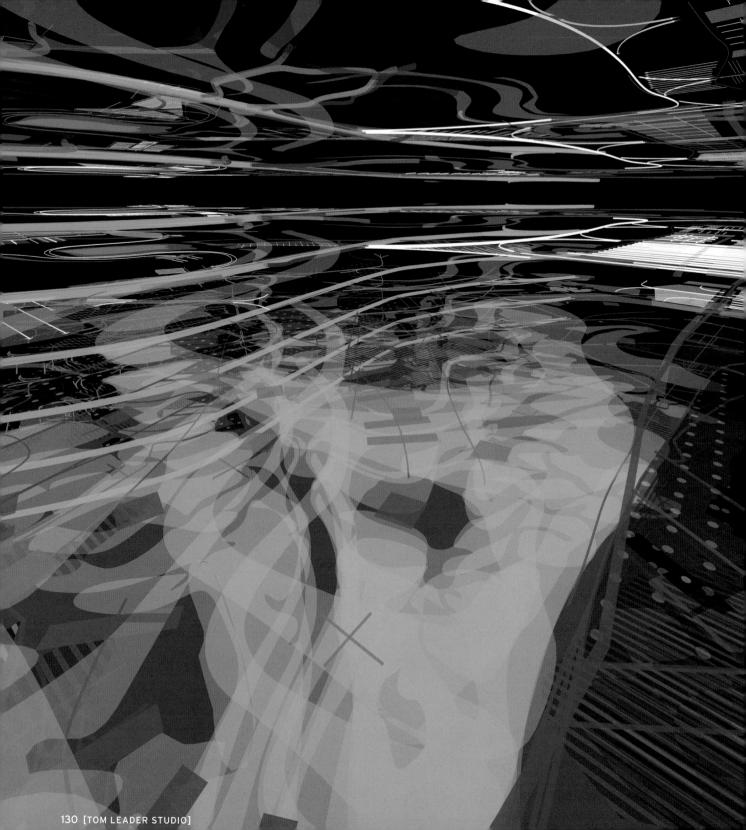

In collaboration with MATHER/DA CUNHA > **FRESH KILLS RESERVE** > STATEN ISLAND, NEW YORK, 2001

m Leader's invitational entry for the 2001 Fresh Kills Landfill to Landscape International Design Competition, hosted by the City of New
rk, questioned ideologically the ability of landfill to return to landscape. After fifty years as the primary disposal site for New York's
rbage, Fresh Kills was closed in March 2001 in response to the objection of local residents in Staten Island. Digital mapping of this vast
te allowed the Studio to formulate and generate a master plan. Their proposal looked at the study of five dynamics found within the site
at most directly lead to its current as well as future nature. These five dynamics—events, datum, experiments, transport zone, and
ges—resulted in a planning resource that would help to deal with a site that defies a fixed program and generate numerous avenues for
ysical design whenever that became appropriate.

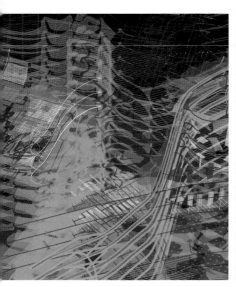

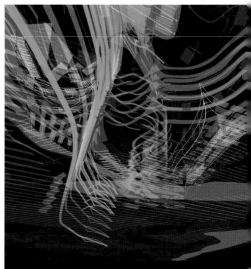

STONE POOL / AZALEA SPRINGS VINEYARD AND RESIDENCE > NAPA VALLEY, CALIFORNIA, 2001-

the hallowed grape-growing soil of the Napa Valley in California, two art collectors operate a prized vineyard and maintain a nineteenth-
ntury farmhouse as their weekend home. A simple linear stone path that connects the forest hillside with the house and the vineyard
came the metaphor for this modern intervention.

Tom Leader Studio proposed a parallel "land bridge" to the east of the walkway as a topographic extrusion that emerges from the
llside. The land bridge acts like a raised plinth and is divided into three zones: a planting field, an open-air pavilion, and a lap pool. Two
ky Spaces" by artist James Turrell were commissioned for this new site; one of them is located within the open-air pavilion's ceiling
ane. A square portion of the ceiling is removed to reveal the sky above, lit at night by a translucent stone floor and a layer of cooling fog
at also serves as a light diffuser. At the end of the lap pool, another Sky Space can only be reached by swimming underwater and sur-
cing in a cube-like grotto bathed in the deep blue light of the sky.

> ARK OF THE WORLD MUSEUM > SAN JOSE, COSTA RICA, 2002

tuated in the heart of the mountainous primary rain forests of Costa Rica, Lynn's design is inspired by the tropical flora and fauna digenous to the country in both its form, color, and symbolism. This highly contextual building also illustrates Lynn's interests in bilateral mmetry and architectural patterning that now can become structural through modes of digital production.

The Ark of the World is an institution that celebrates the ecological diversity, environmental preservation, eco-tourism, and the culral heritage of Costa Rica. The program for the building is a mixture of natural history and contemporary art museums as well as an ology center. The vast site is designed to accommodate the museum's main entrance through a garden of water-filled columns, which uld keep the site cool and moist. The building's rotund form has a central vertical space and a helical stair that rises three stories and rminates in a glass fiber-reinforced fabric-covered canopy from which visitors can view the canopies of the surrounding rain forests. The ound floor extends beyond the massing of the upper portion of the building and unfolds into the landscape, terminating in a stage and nphitheater for outdoor music performances.

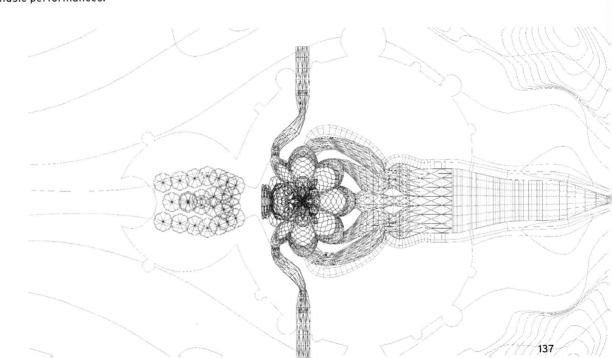

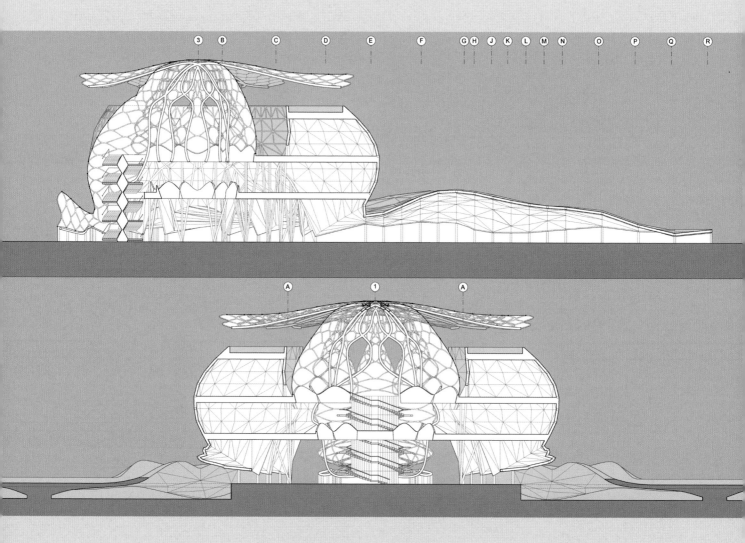

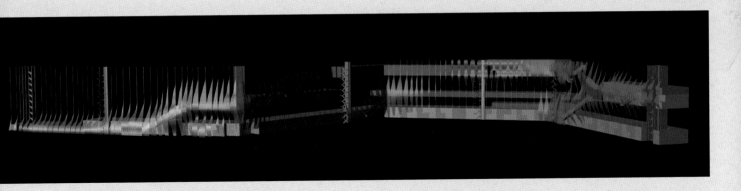

GREG LYNN / FORM > **TRANSFORMATION OF KLEIBURG BLOCK/HOUSING RENOVATION** >

THE AMSTERDAM DISTRICT OF BIJLMERMEER, NETHERLANDS, 2000

his existing five hundred-unit housing block, built in the early 1970s, is located in the outskirts of Amsterdam in the Bijlmermeer neigh-
orhood. These housing blocks are gentrified for a more diverse demographic mixture of people. Lynn's proposal for the Transformation of
leiburg Block is an ideal model for the reuse of this type of building. Half of the units will be renovated and rented while the remaining
50 will be sold as condominiums.

The redistribution of existing spaces and the redesign of public spaces provide neighborhoods with distinct identities. Lynn
chieves this through a mixture of new elevators and escalators that allow the various neighborhoods to puzzle together in a variety of
onfigurations. The new circulation is supported by a series of over 150 uniquely shaped vertical steel trusses, clad in a semi-transparent
tainless-steel fabric, and appears parasitic to the existing housing block. It is through these vertical trusses that new escalators pass and
re supported by the existing concrete structure.

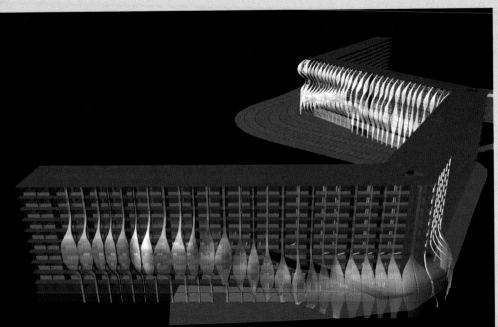

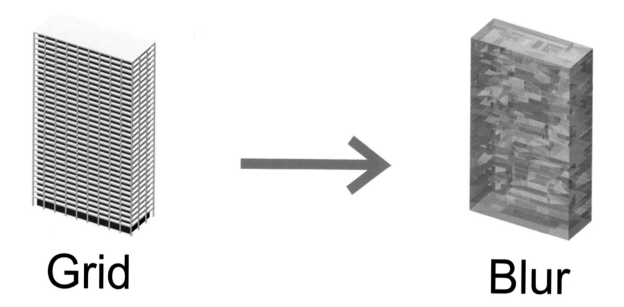

Grid

Blur

EINHOLD MARTIN & KADAMBARI BAXI

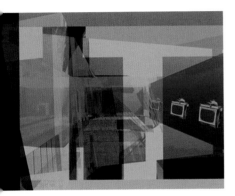  

> ENTROPIA: HOME OFFICE > HOUSTON, TEXAS, 1999

This highly theoretical study looks at an increasingly obsolete architecture—the modern skyscraper—reprogramming it and replacing its skin. The model for this analysis was the 1960 First City National Bank in Houston, Texas, designed by Gordon Bunshaft of Skidmore, wings, and Merrill. The SOM building was chosen for its structural clarity—the frame is expressed on the outside in order to minimize its effect on the interior office space.

Martin Baxi reprogrammed the building into a combination of half "home" and half "office" spaces. The home and office spaces are zoned into two continuous volumes that wrap around each other. The skin of the skyscraper is a glass-clad surface that is transparent in the home space and semi-transparent in the office space. This analysis is then duplicated in the reverse order. Combining all of the generated skins produces an intricate system of skins within skins that visually activates this normative skyscraper. The home and office continually blur the physical, and intellectual, boundaries between each other as they become exposed at the building's internal core and the street facades.

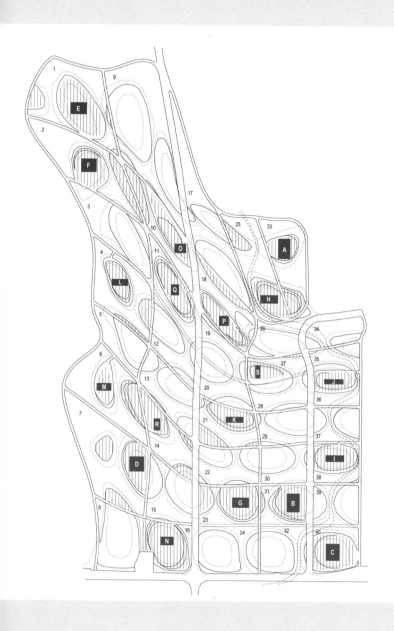

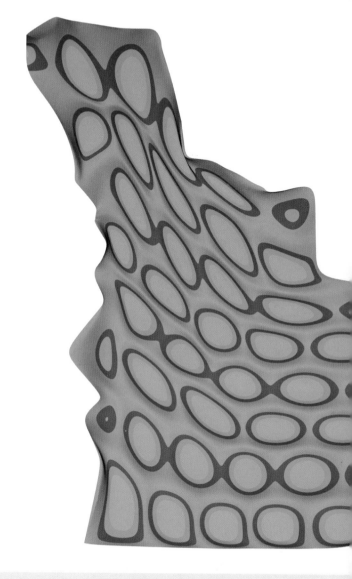

Timeline by Martin + Baxi is a multi-part project that combines analysis and design in an ever-broader sweep through the recent past and the not-too-distant future. Intellectually, its primary purpose is to rethink the city and architecture in a globalized, digital age. The project is a conceptual loop starting with Silicon Valley's architectural and urban logic, which is then excavated, analyzed, imported to Bangalore, and recycled back again to Silicon Valley. This vast ongoing project works on four principles: The Entropy, The Golf Course, The Atrium, and The iMac. The result is The Cisco System that encapsulates the transition from low "pancake" buildings to taller towers, as land values and densities increase. This methodology looks at the redistribution of network channels and the adaptive reuse of existing buildings, as well as the reduction of built architecture for corporate campuses. It also functions as a solution applied to other corporate headquarters such as Intel, Apple, 3Com, Oracle, and Alza.

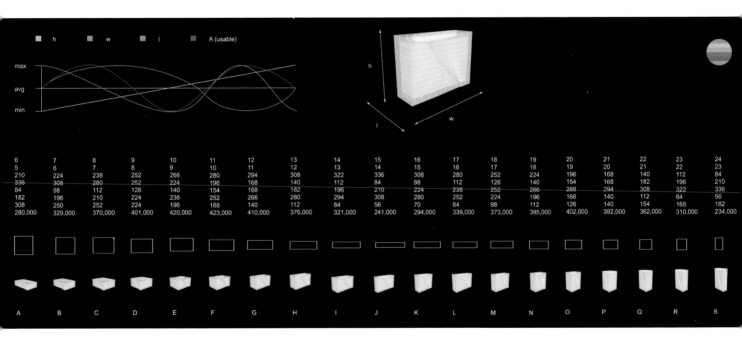

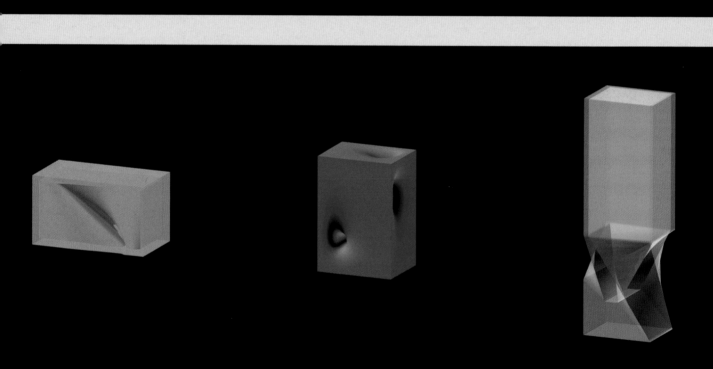

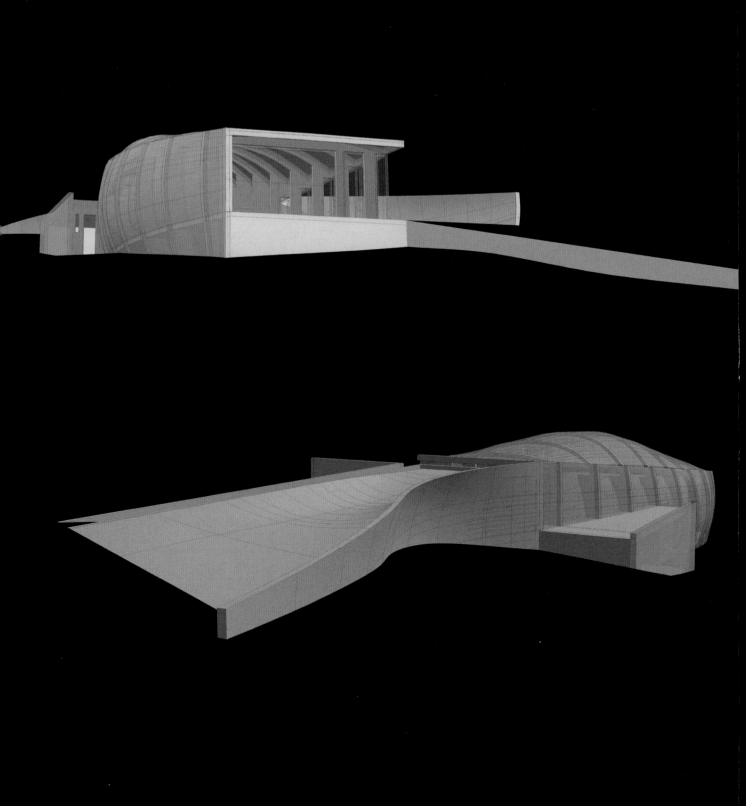

> BIG BELT HOUSE: ON COMPLEX CURVATURE > MEAGHER COUNTY, MONTANA, 2000

The conceptual basis for the Big Belt House stems from Massie's idea of "visual rhyming," which is an exploration to develop a relationship to the landscape that is less object/subject in nature. To achieve this, Massie employed topographies from the site and their geometries and digitally reassembled them to form the primary elements of the interior space, offering back a "visual rhyme" with the actual landscape.

The Big Belt House is achieved through a process of both virtual and actual construction. First, the site topographies are transposed and reconfigured as the initial spatial assembly in the form of a virtual computer model. Then program and structure are folded in, and the overall form is critiqued and synthesized. Massie then uses the sectional condition of the house as a primary element to analyze both the resulting interior space and the articulation of structural possibilities for the house. This results in a digitally filtered rectangular house—with nonrectilinear elements contained within—that is both contextual to its region and Massie's ideology.

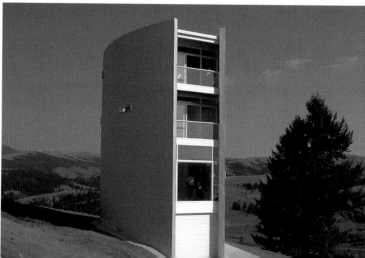

The concept for the Big Sky House stems from the notion of architectural markings that become measurable in a vast landscape. Rather than contouring to the topographical conditions, Massie juxtaposed forms to create relationships between conditions. Here, the house becomes a visual marker between the straight line of the highway and the contrasting mountains. The highway actually curves to circumnavigate the natural barrier of the mountain, which in turn becomes the focus from inside the house. The house is comprised of two very minimal compound curving walls that funnel light inside the dwelling. From the foundation work to the kitchen cabinets and interior walls, all were fabricated from CNC milling processes.

ÜRGEN MAYER H.

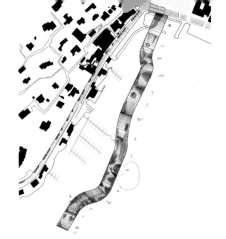

> SEASONSCAPE: ASCONA LAKEFRONT PIER > ASCONA, SWITZERLAND, 1997

asonscape, by Jürgen Mayer H., placed third in the international competition organized by the City of Ascona, Switzerland. The pro-
sed design floats in front of the coast of Ascona, doubling the surface of the seaside promenade as well as creating new infrastructure
r tourism. This new surface—an artificial landmass—is a pontoonscape that oscillates at water level and houses a ferry terminal with var-
us tourist programs. The structural concept for Seasonscape resembles a human spine. All pontoons are connected by compressible
bber joints and anchored to the bottom of the lake. Surface formations can be modified for different seasons as well as temporal func-
onal needs. A lightly structured flexible skin covers the pontoons and houses the upper programmatic layer.

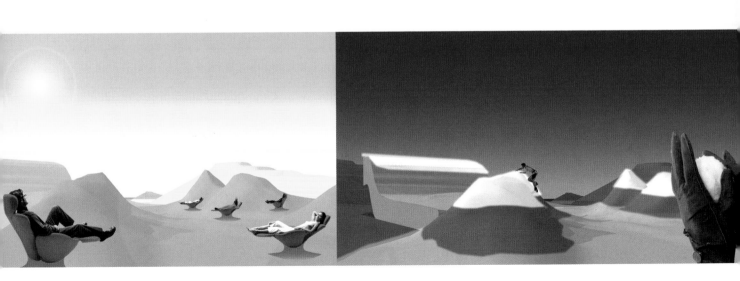

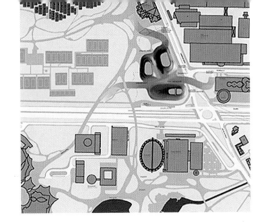

JÜRGEN MAYER H. › BMW EVENT AND DELIVERY CENTER › MUNICH, GERMANY, 2001

rgen Mayer H.'s design competition entry for the BMW Event and Delivery Center proposes a building that is a large event space and the
ntral "activator" of this vast BMW complex. Situated between the BMW tower, museum, and the Olympic Park, the BMW Event and
livery Center fuses multiple forms of leisure, entertainment, economics, and sports.

To emphasize the building's role as a social condenser, Mayer extends large ramps out from the building into the public spaces of
ese adjacent structures. This vast bloblike building also contains a public roofscape with skylights that allow visitors to view events that
e taking place inside and outside the building.

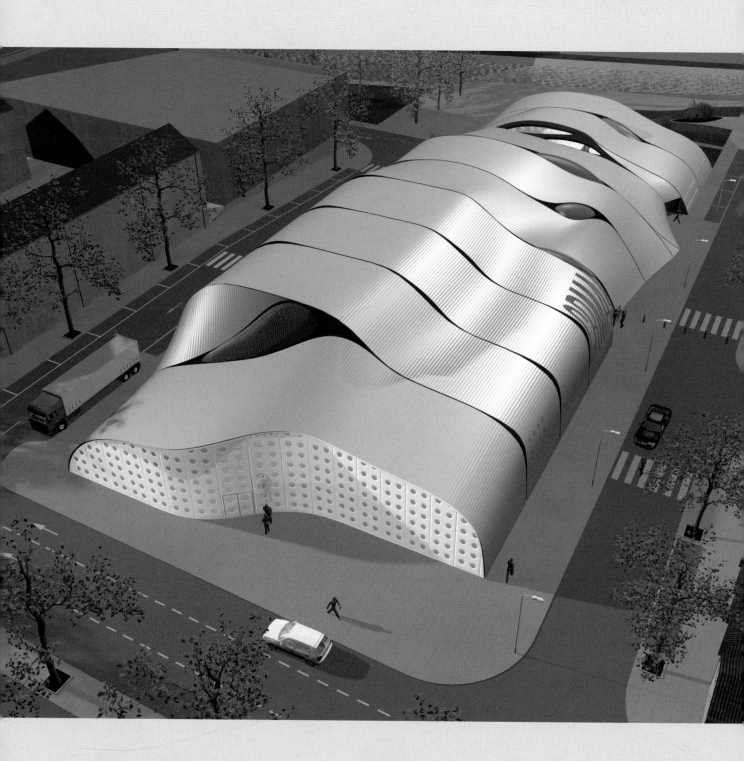

> CRMA POP MUSIC CENTER > NANTES, FRANCE, 2002

e CRMA Pop Music Center is composed of a series of equidistant bands collectively assembled into one complete undulating building rm, signifying its civic presence. Ideologically, the equal band surfaces become deformed, bent, and torn to create the main entrance, ylights, and double-height interior spaces. Lars Spuybraek's work seeks to merge the concepts of porosity with curved surfaces. In this ethodology it is more logical for holes and curvature to co-merge and generate architectural form. The employment of holes, however, is t a reductive process, but rather a positive condition that allows the perforated plane to literally become a structurally curved surface. uybraek refers to this process of integration as "machining architecture." The CRMA Pop Music Center is an example of this methodol- y in action. By distorting, folding, bending, and tearing into the equal bands of surface, Spuybraek creates multiple subsurfaces and reg- trations that allow the program to encode itself onto the building's form.

NOX > MAISON FOLIE > LILLE, FRANCE, 2001

Maison Folie is an old textile factory that has been renovated into an arts-related building and an adjacent new building to house a
rt hall, foyer, and sound studio. The new concert hall building is visually in keeping with the adjacent, historic urban fabric. The main
 of the new building, however, is clad in an undulating stainless-steel mesh material—traditionally employed for conveyer belt sur-
n factories. This mesh facade reflects the sun during the day and at night is illuminated from within. NOX refers to openings on this
e as a "lake strategy," when a flat surface intersects with a curved one.

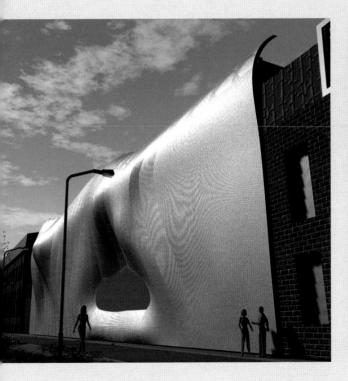

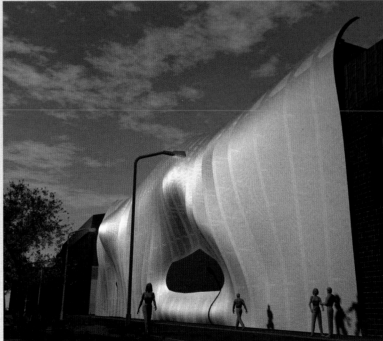

OCEAN D

ROBERT ELFER, KEVIN CESPEDES, WADE STEVENS, AND TOM VEREBES

> GRAD_8 INSTALLATION > GRAZ, AUSTRIA, 2002

Designed for the Latent Utopias exhibition, curated by Zaha Hadid and Patrik Schumacher for the Landesmuseum Joanneum, grad_8 installation encodes Ocean D's ideology and is a small sample of the visual complexities that can be realized through digitally filtered responses to criteria.

For Ocean D, the installation exemplifies digital's new role of enabling material production to offer increasing variation and control over highly complex geometries. The installation—grad_8—is comprised of five different digitally produced objects that were assigned a limited set of site-specific performance criteria within a constraining volume. All five scripted operations are configured by ten splines. The splines are then offset and rotated, causing variable distributions of these splines within each constraining volume. A secondary set of splines is incorporated to generate a series of strands that negotiate the nearest intersecting splines to make rigid the loose lattice. The horizontal steel tube splines and vertically wrapped perforated steel sheets collaborate to configure a highly graduated density of material across the sequences of the five objects. Several architectural conditions result from this operation including possible seating, shelving, a projection screen, thresholds, and porous enclosures as well as physical boundaries.

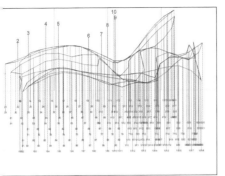 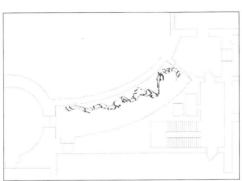 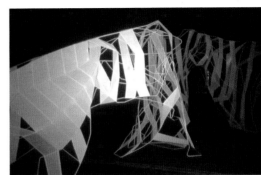

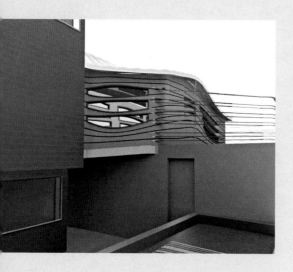

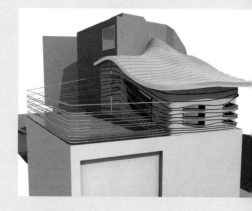

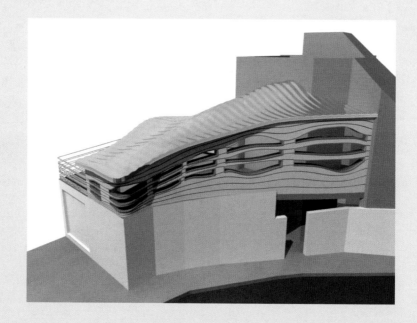

J House is a conversion and extension of a late-1970s modern house on an already limited site. The extension is comprised of a bridge
that spans over an existing entry and leads to a new pavilion that will be used as a studio, children's play area, and guest facilities. The
multipurpose pavilion's roof structure is an assembly of metal buttresses that span from the load-bearing brick walls of the existing
house to the perimeter of the new enclosure. The result is a visually undulating roof configuration that is mediated by a secondary
structure of timber joists. The overall perimeter shape of the new pavilion is demarcated by a series of horizontal windows of varying
size that wrap the building.

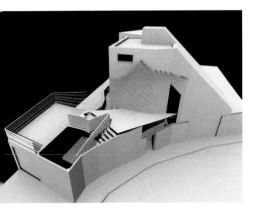
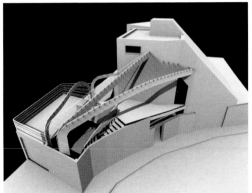
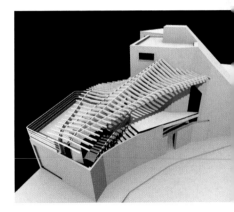

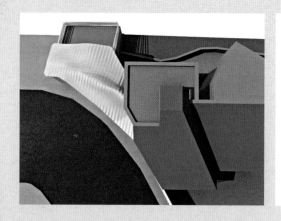

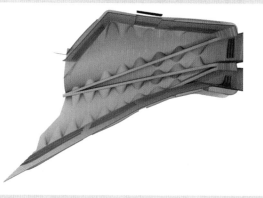

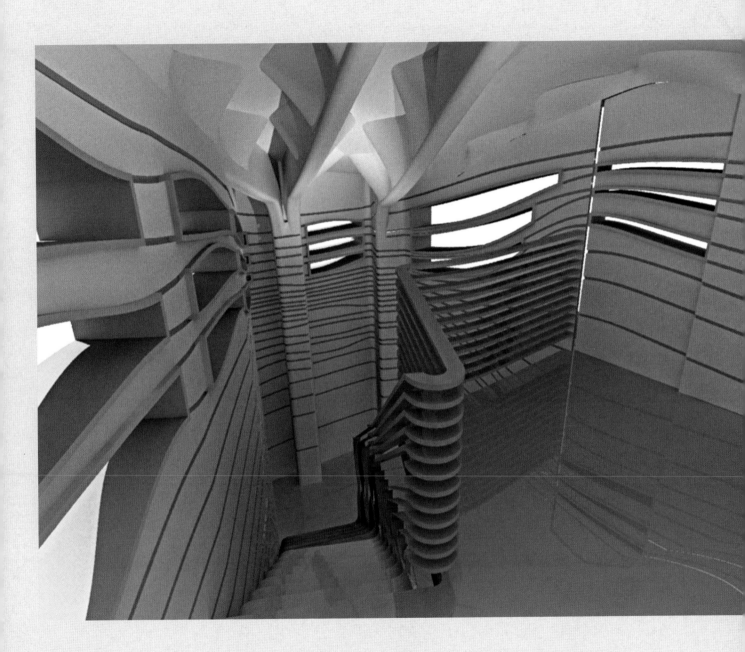

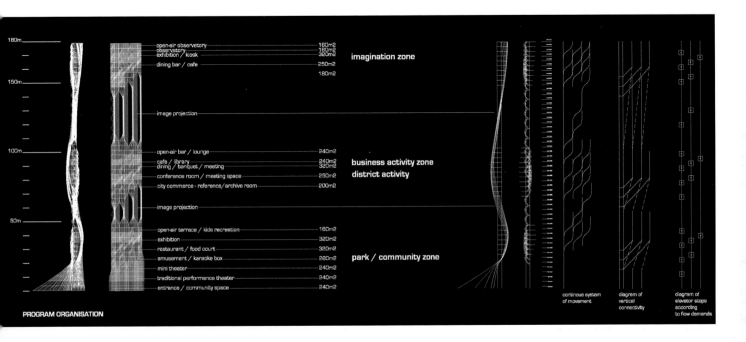

open-air observatory — 180m2
observatory — 180m2
exhibition / kiosk — 320m2
dining bar / cafe — 250m2
— 180m2

imagination zone

image projection

open-air bar / lounge — 240m2
cafe / library — 240m2
dining / banquet / meeting — 320m2
conference room / meeting space — 250m2
city commerce - reference/archive room — 200m2

business activity zone
district activity

image projection

open-air terrace / kids recreation — 160m2
exhibition — 320m2
restaurant / food court — 320m2
amusement / karaoke box — 280m2
mini theater — 240m2
traditional performance theater — 240m2
entrance / community space — 240m2

park / community zone

continuous system of movement

diagram of vertical connectivity

diagram of elevator stops according to flow demands

PROGRAM ORGANISATION

> NEW BUSAN TOWER > BUSAN, SOUTH KOREA, 2002

Marcelo Spina's competition entry for the Busan Tower introduces an architecture that maintains a familiarity with the systems and forces that shape everyday material life. The design for this new tower is a vertical infrastructure that is both a heterogeneous object and an extension of the city. On another level, this minimal filigree-like extruded tower can also be seen as a material incarnation of its variable vector movements. A series of random event conditions derived from the junction of its shifting trajectories are visible in the tower's intersecting surfaces.

The Busan Tower consists of three zones. The upper zones are designated for global activities, whereas the lower zones are used for local activities. Although many different programs are disposed throughout the tower's floor plates, the flexible circulation system allows for interaction, flow, and mixing between programmed conditions.

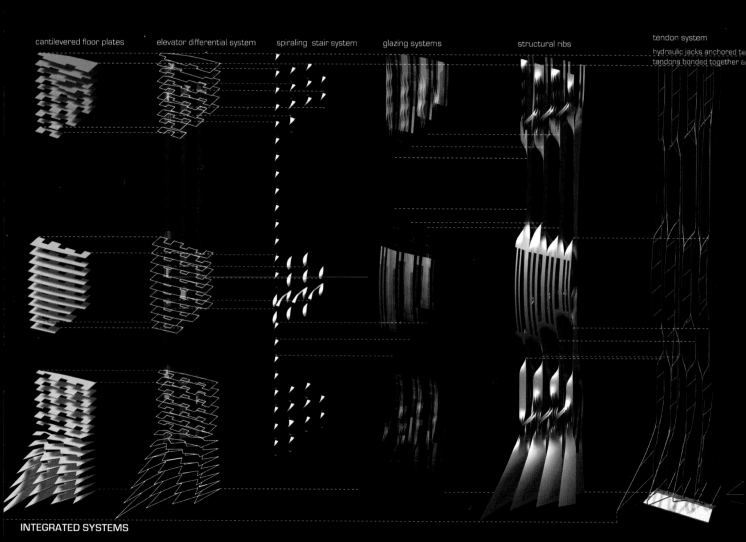

cantilevered floor plates   elevator differential system   spiraling stair system   glazing systems   structural ribs   tendon system

hydraulic jacks anchored t
tendons bonded together a

INTEGRATED SYSTEMS

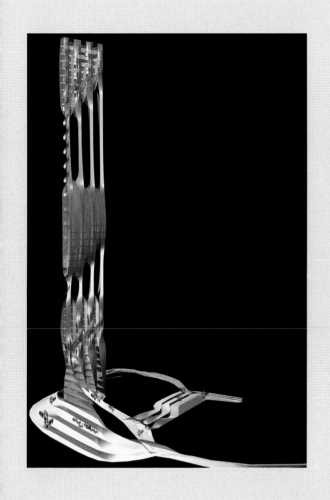

Marcelo Spina's proposal for the Tomihiro Museum of Shi-ga tries to create a quiet but active environment where poems and watercolor can be appreciated in the close context of the surrounding natural environment. The museum is a scenic event that incorporates th topography of the site. The project attempts to unify art and life in a new way by promoting public and material vitalism through th understanding of the work of Tomihiro. This is achieved by both the material form and strategic layout of the museum. The building is con nected via a continuous circuit loop that maintains the connectivity throughout the site, actively engaging the visitors. Through th employment of spaces with slightly sloped surfaces, the loop becomes the structural event around the galleries and their ancillary space

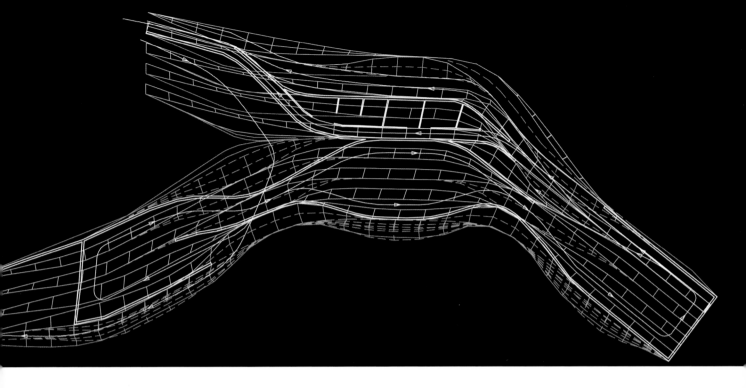

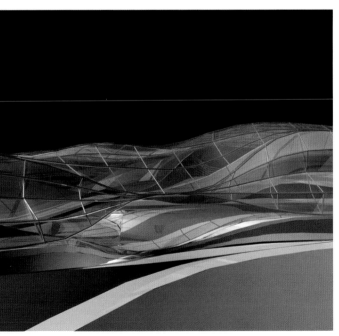

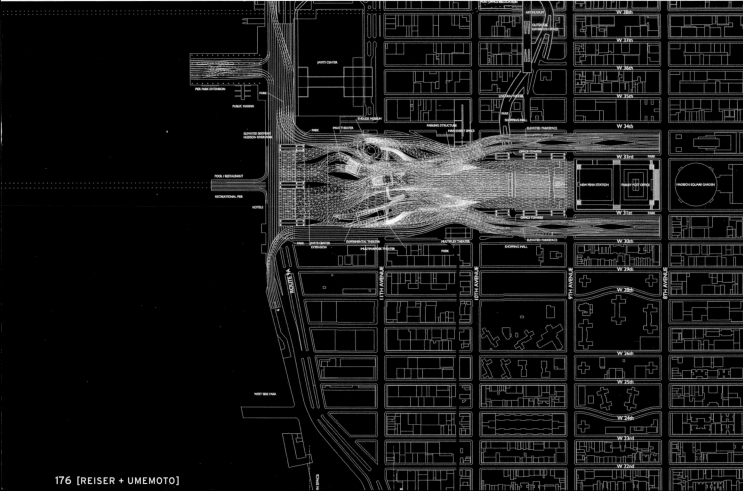

REISER + UMEMOTO

ESSIE REISER & NANAKO UMEMOTO

> WEST SIDE CONVERGENCE PROJECT > NEW YORK, NEW YORK, 1999

Reiser + Umemoto's submission for the Design of Cities competition, sponsored by the International Foundation for the Canadian Centre or Architecture (IFCCA), conveys the impression of a vast natural landscape punctuated by skyscrapers.

Their competition proposal assumes a Manhattan site, spanning the area from 30th to 34th Streets and from Eighth Avenue to he West Side Highway. Close examination reveals a design for an enormous structure comprised of multiple levels. The upper level includes an interior park; the lower level provides access to trains as well as discretely located concessions and commuter conveniences. The vast rolling spaceframe roof visually reads as an unfolding landscape.

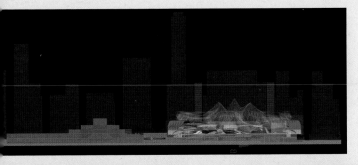

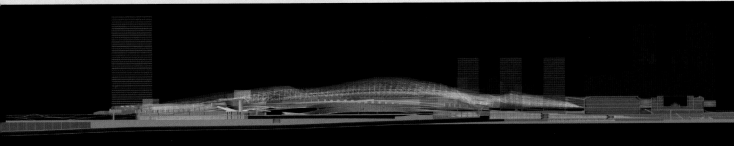

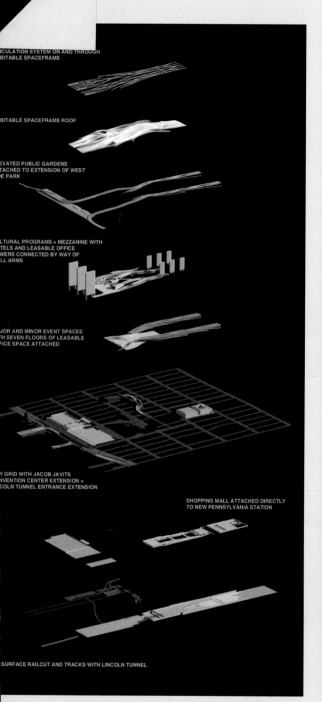

CIRCULATION SYSTEM ON AND THROUGH
HABITABLE SPACEFRAME

HABITABLE SPACEFRAME ROOF

ELEVATED PUBLIC GARDENS
ATTACHED TO EXTENSION OF WEST
SIDE PARK

CULTURAL PROGRAMS + MEZZANINE WITH
HOTELS AND LEASABLE OFFICE
TOWERS CONNECTED BY WAY OF
MALL ARMS

MAJOR AND MINOR EVENT SPACES
WITH SEVEN FLOORS OF LEASABLE
OFFICE SPACE ATTACHED

CITY GRID WITH JACOB JAVITS
CONVENTION CENTER EXTENSION +
LINCOLN TUNNEL ENTRANCE EXTENSION

SHOPPING MALL ATTACHED DIRECTLY
TO NEW PENNSYLVANIA STATION

SURFACE RAILCUT AND TRACKS WITH LINCOLN TUNNEL

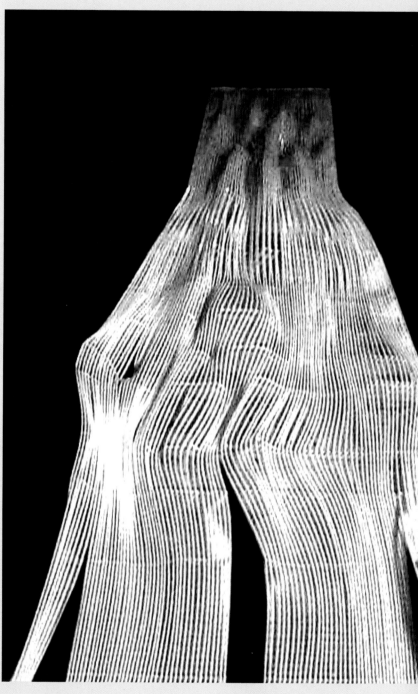

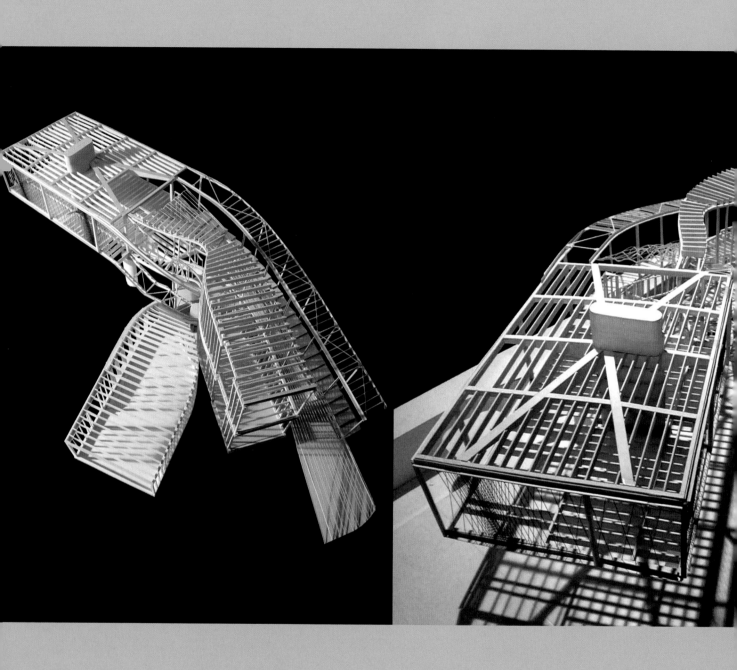

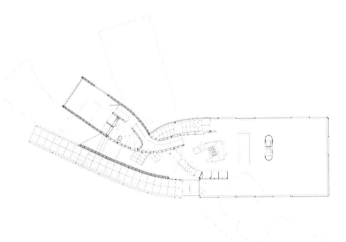

REISER + UMEMOTO > SAGAPONAC HOUSE > SAGAPONACK, NEW YORK, 2002

ocated on a two-acre wooded site within a subdivision, Reiser + Umemoto's design addresses the synthesis of two potentially antagonis-
ic conditions: the twentieth-century model of the house as a discrete pavilion and the formal as well as organizational strategy that pro-
notes no clear boundary between house and landscape, or inside and outside.

Revisiting Ludwig Mies van der Rohe's conception of universal space, Reiser + Umemoto augmented a pure rectangular glass pavilion
orm by twisting it and creating separation between the public and private character of the rectangle. The horizontally positioned glass-
nclosed living/dining room is anchored to the site by a centrally located fireplace from which this form cantilevers; the vertically disposed
ondition is the private location of two bedrooms. A staircase is literally woven between these torqued, horizontal (public) and vertical (pri-
ate) spatial conditions. The result is a new methodology and architectural paradigm for the glass house of the twenty-first century.

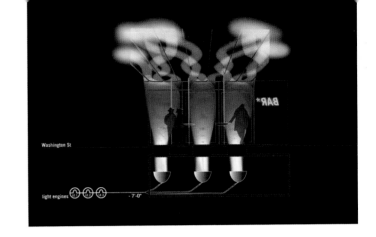

> NOAH BAR > NEW YORK, NEW YORK, 2001

The Noah bar was designed for a defunct cooler located in the Meat-Packing District—a neighborhood that formally serviced the meat-packing industry but has now become a trend-setting location for galleries, boutiques, and late night restaurants. Instead of gutting the space of any trace of its historical past, Lindy Roy used it as a metaphor to create one of the most dynamic contextual settings for a bar. This was achieved by merging multi-functional interpretations, fiber-optics, and standard, off-the-shelf equipment for transporting meat with the notion of "convertible space."

Roy refurbished and reconfigured the system typically used for the transportation of meat from truck to freezer. These vertical mobile poles became the locations for resin tables and suspended chaises that could be completely reconfigured depending on the event. The space over this suspended horizontal metal work contains braided fiber-optics that rise up from the basement in the back of the space, over the apparatus, and terminate at the entrance, spelling out the function of the space.

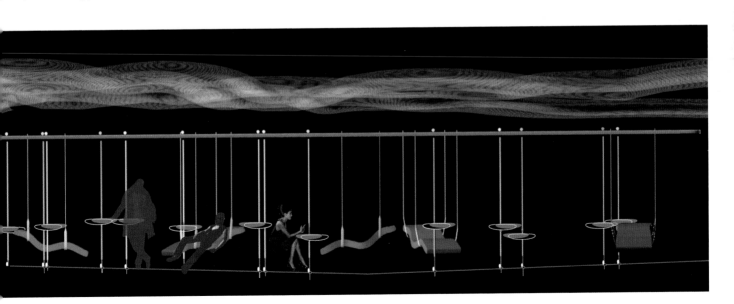

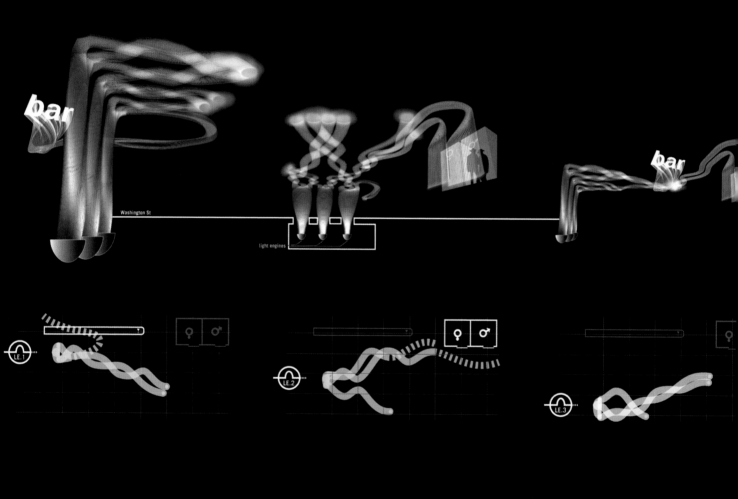

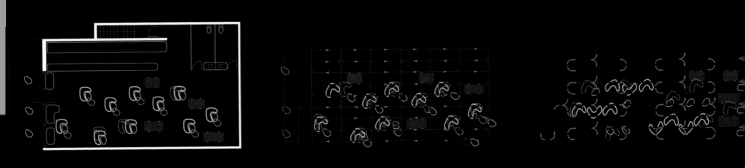

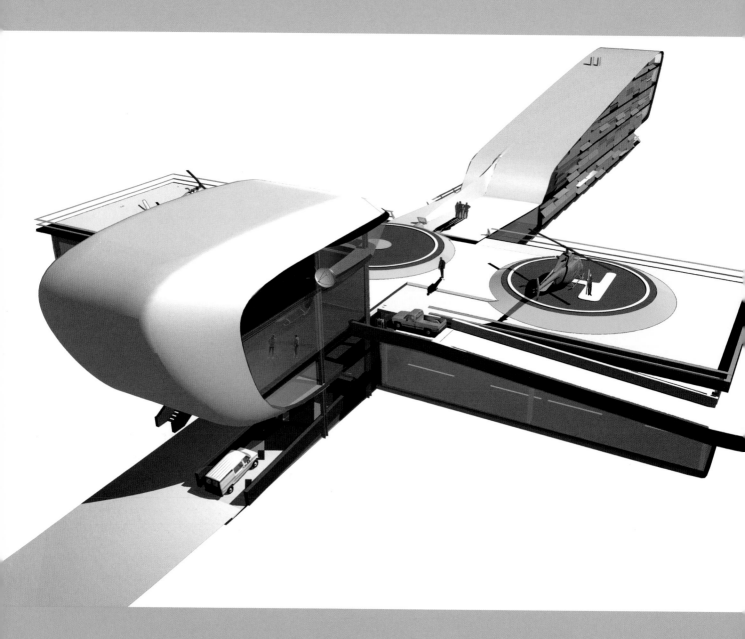

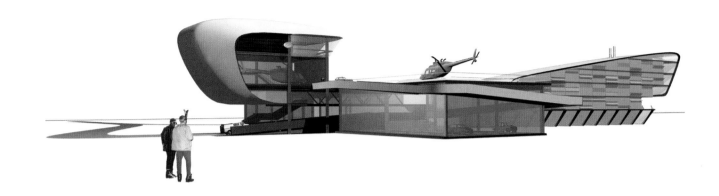

ROY > WIND RIVER LODGE > CHUGACH MOUNTAIN RANGE, ALASKA, 2001

e Wind River Lodge is an extreme skiing facility in southern Alaska. Roy employs a folded form to create a sinuous structure that is
perimental and metanarrative in form and innovative in resolution. Conceptually, the building's surface bends back onto itself at either
d to create a twenty-six-room hotel and a shape Roy calls "the ski helmet" that contains the control tower in one half and a bar in the
her. These spaces are separated by a wall but share one continuous countertop. Transversing this sculptural ensemble is a simple rec-
ngle that provides space for three helipads and physically connects these two forms. The monolithic shape of the lodge will employ gal-
nized steel extrusions, fabricated through digital manufacturing, trucked to the site in components, and then assembled.

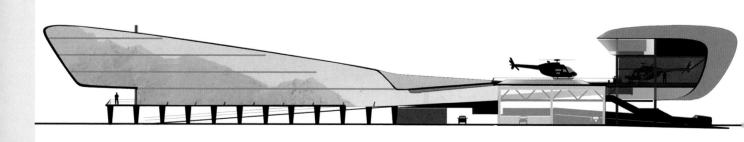

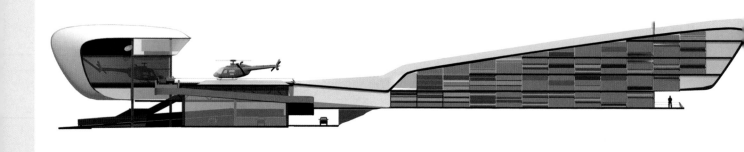

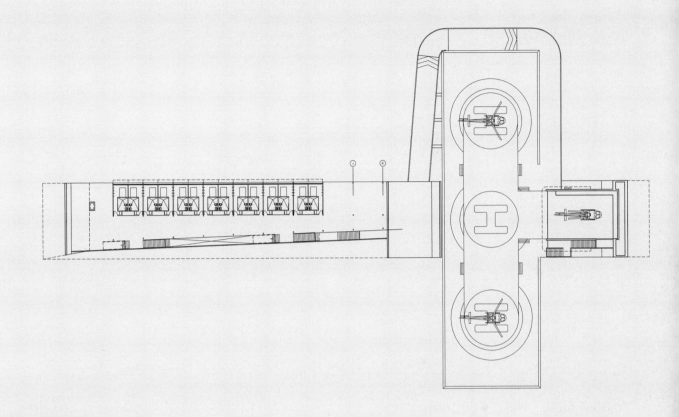

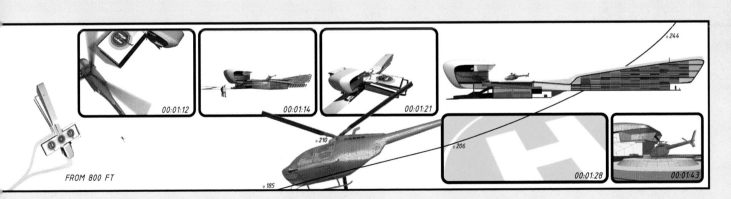

FROM 800 FT

00:01:12

00:01:14

00:01:21

o 244

o 210

o 206

o 185

00:01:28

00:01:43

> 24/7 HOTEL ROOM > PROTOTYPE, 2002

oel Sanders's 24/7 Hotel Room is a prototype with the objective of retooling the template of a traditional hotel room (12' X 24') into an pulent, productive 24/7 space. Building off of his earlier proposal for the Five-Minute Bathroom, commissioned by *Wallpaper* magazine in 000, Sanders expands this concept into the complete hotel room experience. His design looks at the hotel room condition similarly to Le orbusier's ideology for his apartment units, conceptually plugged into the larger framework of their building.

The 24/7 Hotel Room would be fabricated from fiberglass components that comprise two separate units but can also function as ne suite. By zoning the hotel room space, Sanders has visually and literally folded functions together; office/seating area, bed/conversa-on pit, spa/bathroom, and a floor-to-ceiling fitness center merge to create an overall space driven by fitness/efficiency that is emblem-ic of the ideal twenty-first-century hotel experience.

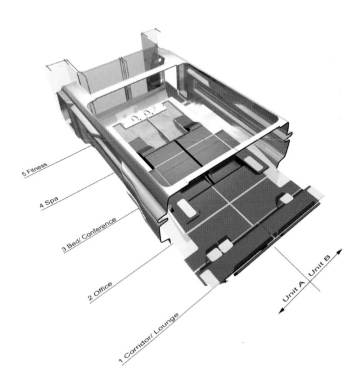

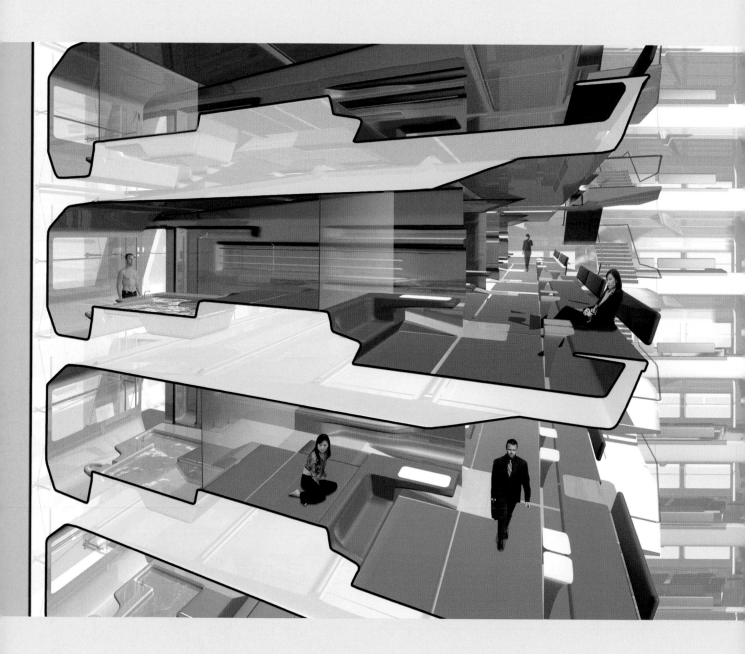

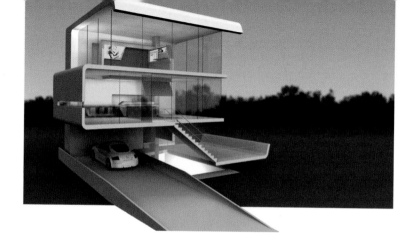

JOEL SANDERS > ACCESS HOUSE > ST. SIMONS ISLAND, GEORGIA, 200

Designed as a weekend retreat, the Access House has floor-to-ceiling glass walls with vast views to the water beyond. While the twentieth century glass house has historically been the site for social spectacle and voyeurism, the twenty-first-century notion of this same typology has inverted to surveillance and safety. Sanders's Access House addresses this dichotomy of spectacle and surveillance. Within th mostly glass house is an "E:core"–a digital device similar in concept to a telescope–located at the core of the building. Strategically placed surveillance cameras dispersed throughout the house transmit images to the E:core that can be observed via screens embedded i the surfaces of all the floors and vertically connected throughout the house.

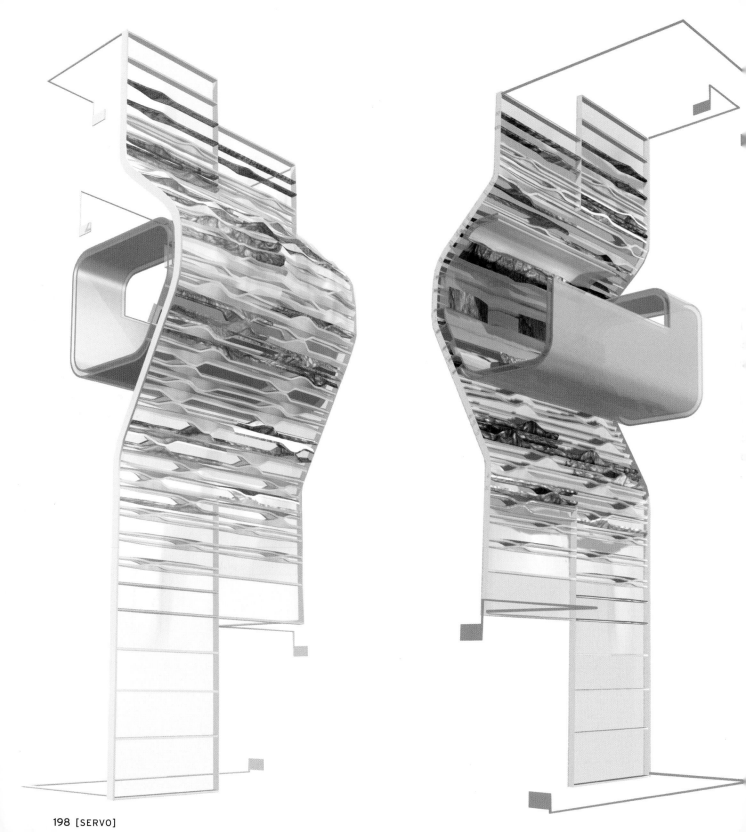

ERVO

DAVID ERDMAN, MARCELYN GOW, ULRIKA KARLSSON, CHRIS PERRY

ERVO's Lobbi_ports is a speculative project that sees the future of hotel lobbies as cultural terminals or ports of entry for cities. While these proposed hotel lobbies appear parasitic to the existing hotel buildings, they would function as public urban living rooms as well as cultural destinations for tourists. These hotel lobbies are concealed by an "implanted" curtainwall that carries both people and soft infrastructure. The system re-wires and redistributes the circuits of existing towers bought by new hotel corporations.

These expanded "wall" lobby spaces are situated vertically, constructing an urban condition that attaches to the building's exterior and rises up the hotel tower. The newly implanted enclosure system is conceptualized as a physical software that provides these spaces with light, sound, and video. Using programmable LED sheets, video streams would pass through the curtain-wall cavity at various speeds. The implanted curtainwall would also simultaneously redistribute the cultural and pedestrian character of the tower for public information and use.

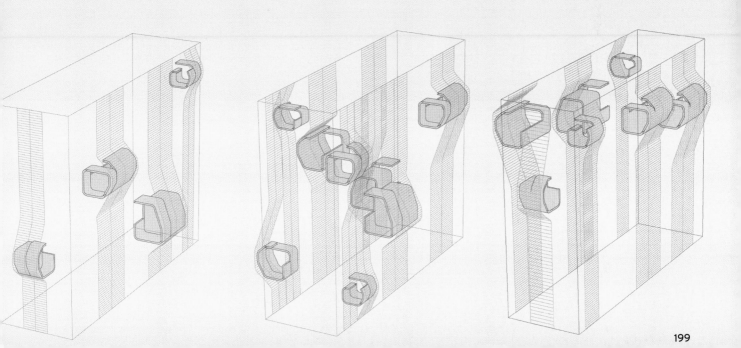

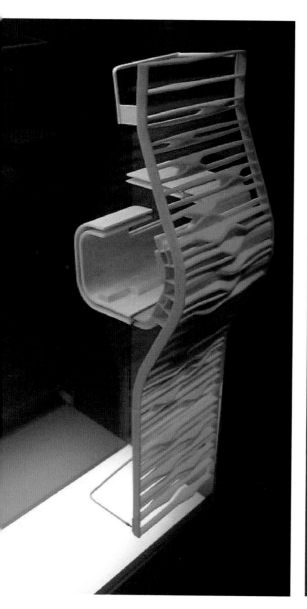

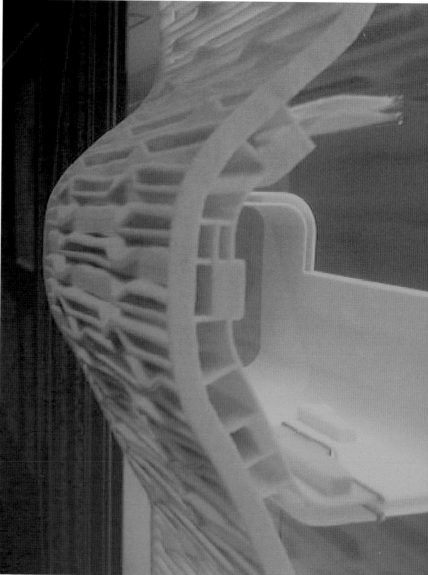

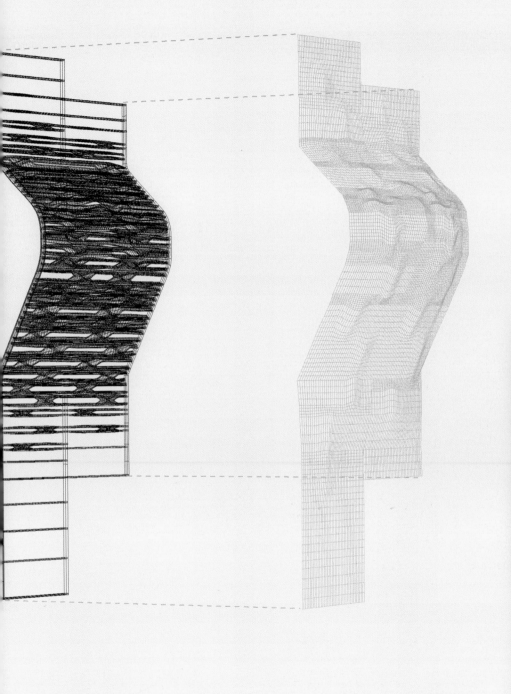
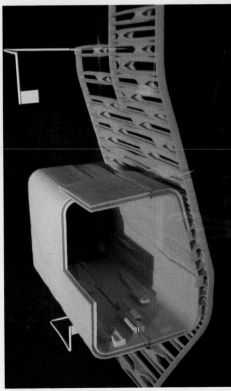

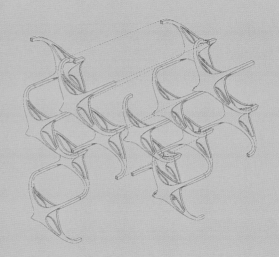

SERVO > LATTICE ARCHIPE_LOGICS > 2002

his interactive spatial matrix by SERVO—Lattice Archipe_logics—illustrates the degree to which digitally literate designers are blurring he boundaries between design, fabrication, and interactive motion-audio-lighting technologies. The overall assembly of this reconfigrable installation is a series of non-figuratively patterned components that illuminate the space and are emblematic of a return to serialty in modern architecture through digital augmentation. The project contains approximately fifty-two pressure formed, translucent, white plastic modules (each one is made up of two forms), an algorithmically relayed LED system, and a surround-sound system.

The Lattice Archipe_logics both passively and actively participates in the interchanges with the gallery environment and visitors. Suspended cellular objects are embedded with motion sensors, lighting, and speaker technologies hence responding to a wide range of physical movement through them by mapping the path of the visitor through sound and light recognition.

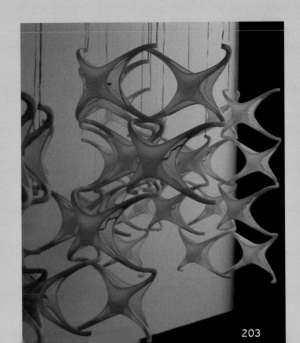

CHRISTOPHER SHARPLES, WILLIAM SHARPLES, COREN SHARPLES, KIMBERLY HOLDEN, & GREGG PASQUARELLI

> DUNESCAPE / MOMA / P.S. 1 > LONG ISLAND CITY, NEW YORK, 2000

A beach metaphor inspired SHoP's design for this temporary structure in P.S. 1 Contemporary Art Center's outdoor courtyard. The tilting, rolling surface of the blob-shaped installation morphs from roof to wall to bench to boardwalk. Characteristics of common beach elements—cabana, beach chair, umbrella, boogie board, and surf—were incorporated into the installation's design.

Dunescape was built from six thousand two-by-two cedar strips varying from eight to twelve feet in length. Three-dimensional computer drawings, printed at a 1:1 scale, served as templates to build the cedar-framed structures, which were then bolted together to create the overall pavilion.

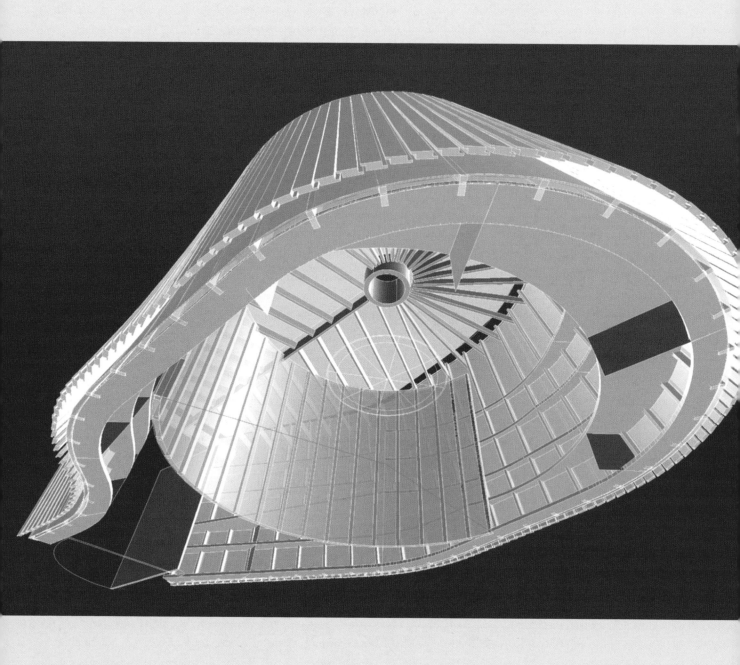

SHOP > MITCHELL PARK: CAMERA OBSCURA > GREENPORT, NEW YORK, 2002

The Camera Obscura building is one of several by SHoP at Mitchell Park, including their recently completed Carousel House. Through an optical lens and a mirror, a live image of the camera's surroundings is projected onto a flat, circular table that is raised or lowered to adjust focal depth; hence, the building is conceived of and operated as a camera. This notion is manifested through the camera's architecture, from its movable components and materials to its placement in Mitchell Park. The camera lens can focus on elements in or out of the park and to the marina beyond as far as Shelter Island.

Entirely designed on a three-dimensional computer model, the construction of the mysterious camera building is communicated as a kit of custom parts accompanied by a set of instructions. The structure is made primarily of aluminum and steel components that are laser-cut directly from digital files, with markings for ease of fabrication, and clad in milled planks that produce a warped exterior skin. The beauty of this design is twofold: its digital conception and its sinuous form, produced by repetitive milling and characteristic of the fourteenth-century mechanics that gave us the camera obscura.

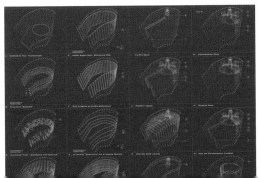

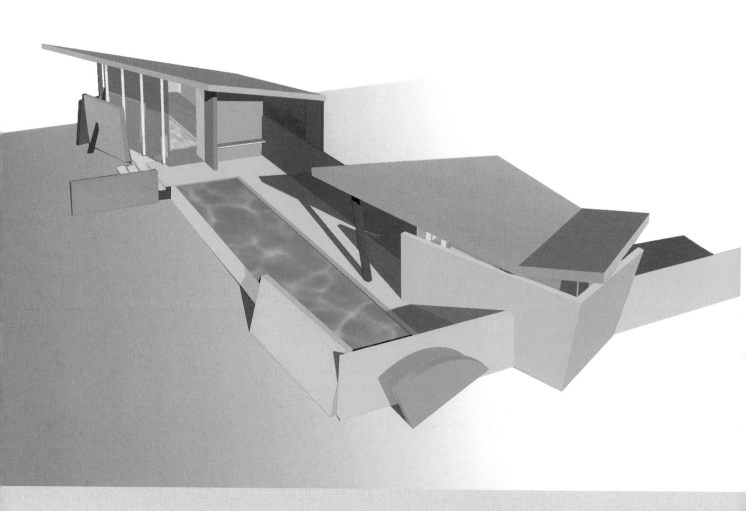

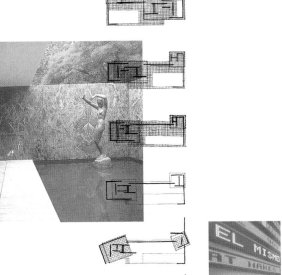

E V O L U T I O N

> SHELTER ISLAND PAVILION > SHELTER ISLAND, NEW YORK, 2000-

Designed as a weekend retreat, this 980-square-foot glass-enclosed structure appears much larger. Comprised of two small glass-enclosed forms, separated by a lap pool and wrapped by a fractured perimeter wall, the pavilion with canted roof is a study in contrasting geometries and colors.

Stamberg Aferiat modeled their design—in plan—after Ludwig Mies van der Rohe's 1929 Barcelona Pavilion, an icon of the modern box in architecture. However, they flipped the plan end-to-end to work with site. Then they digitally twisted it—in plan as well as section—to open the structure to prevailing views. Computer software also enabled them to test and manipulate different color combinations to achieve the bold palette of this vibrant, digitally-produced retreat.

213

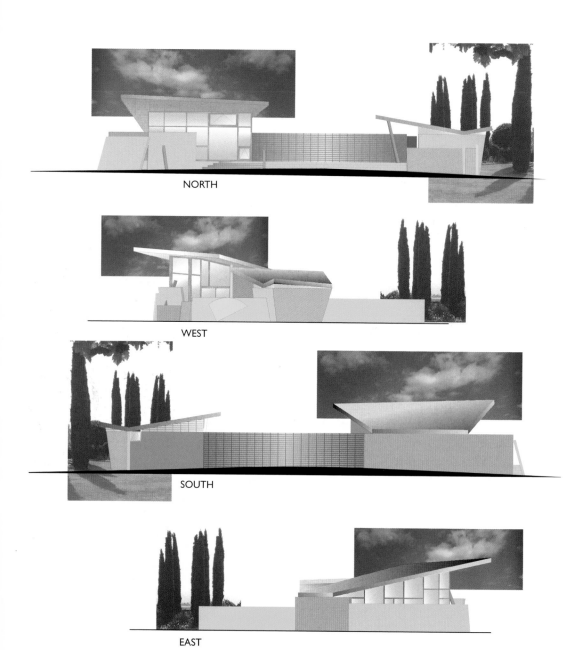

NORTH

WEST

SOUTH

EAST

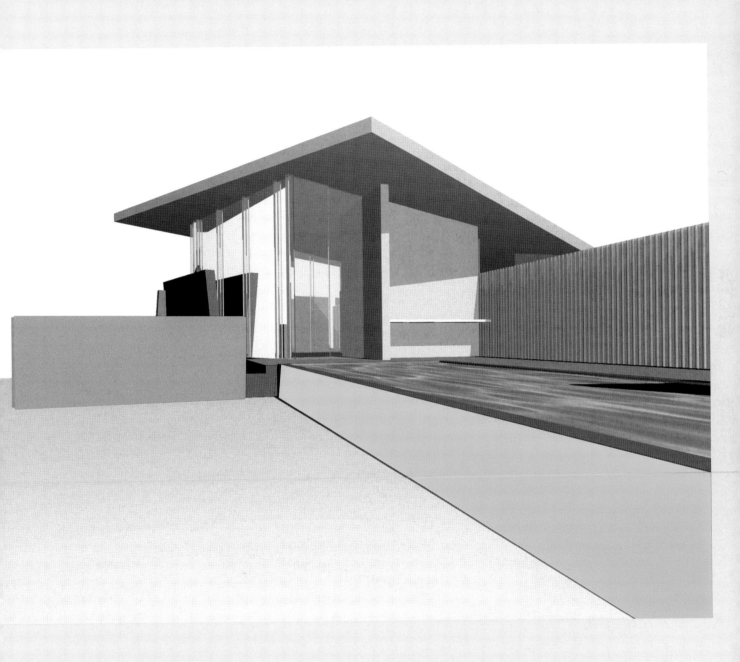

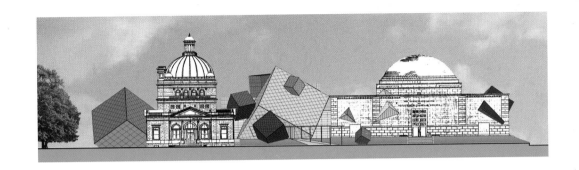

STAMBERG AFERIAT > PITTSBURGH CHILDREN'S MUSEUM > PITTSBURGH, PENNSYLVANIA, 2000

Stamberg Aferiat looked at various color value studies for each surface in relationship to one another to produce a design infused with color, always rendering the building in shade and shadow in this Pittsburgh Children's Museum invitation competition entry. The site for this new expanded facility is literally situated between two historical buildings that will become components of the new museum. Stamberg Aferiat's proposal inserted a series of simple geometric forms that are canted and appear almost randomly placed. To heighten this playfulness and juxtapose its historical contexts, they employed an abundance of color integral to its form. They use color in a very unorthodox way, broadening the discussion of color theory and its role in visual literacy.

A variety of studies in color and proportion were produced to illustrate a shade and shadow relationship that would allow the forms to always appear as if it were actually light outside. Through digital technology, the color values are adjusted to reflect and achieve the ideal condition, and those files are sent directly to a paint manufacturer for production.

> PRAGUE HOUSE > PRAGUE, CZECH REPUBLIC, 2002

Responding to a site located in preservation forest in Prague, adjacent to a steep hill on the property (no construction is permitted on the hill), SYSTEMSarchitects placed the house in a sloped relationship–figuratively and literally–to its topography. The result is a simple yet highly contextual design. This four-plus bedroom house is vast in size but appears smaller in scale due to its vertical orientation adjacent to the hill. Bending, fracturing, and slightly twisting elements of the house's massing generate an assembly that is digitally contextualized at the exterior without significant deformation of the interiors.

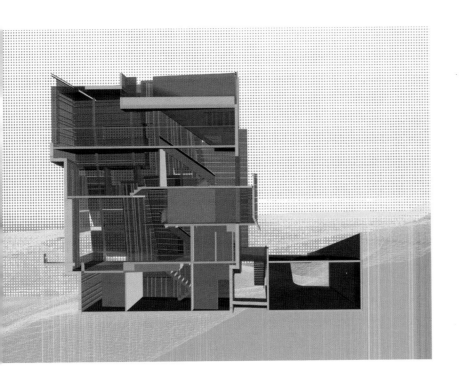

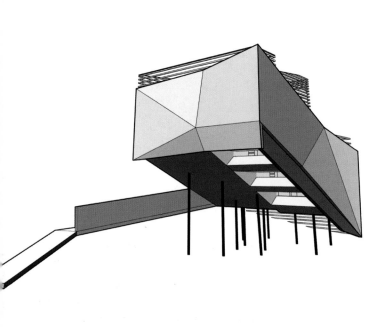

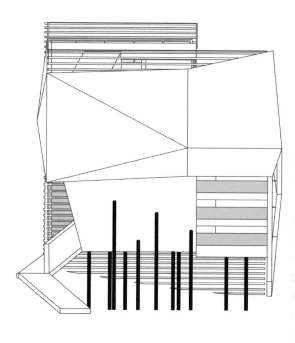

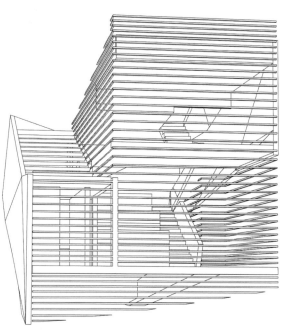

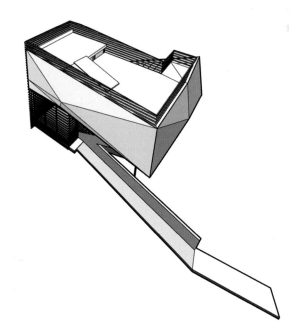

SYSTEMSARCHITECTS > WELLFLEET GUEST HOUSE > CAPE COD, MASSACHUSETTS, 2002

The Guest House is situated on a tree-covered rise 130 feet above Newcomb Hollow Beach. The one-acre site already has an existing main house, however, the new guest house's program is vast, including sleeping areas for eight guests, common area with kitchen, two bathrooms, roof deck, and outdoor shower. While the program reads like a weekend house, SYSTEMSarchitects' design collapses all of these desired conditions into one simple fractured rectangular guest house. A horizontally disposed sun screen wraps the back of the house, which is mostly floor-to-ceiling glass. The back and entrance side of the house reveals its fractured, segmented, torqued upward form. Its aesthetic beauty is pushed further by having this complex form raised off the ground and supported by a series of columns, accessible only by a ramped entrance way. The notion of a simple weekend retreat today can be as complex as a large year-round home; however, SYSTEMSarchitects, through digital torquing and revisiting the sectional characteristic of the modern house, generates a new model for the digitally literate to follow.

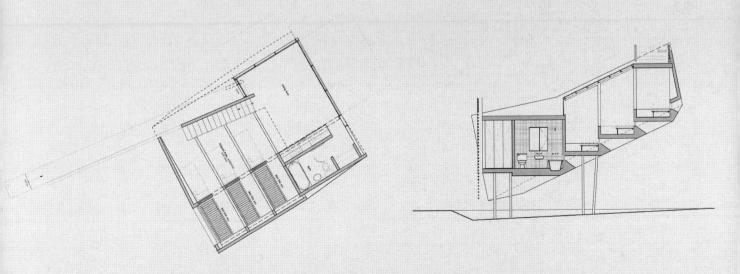

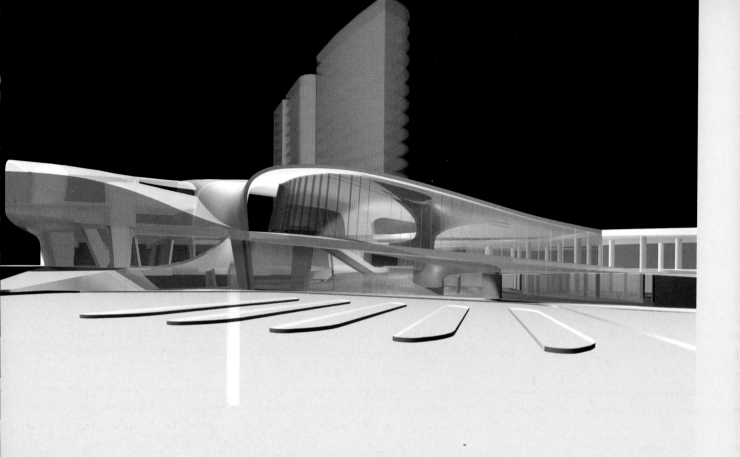

BEN VAN BERKEL & CAROLINE BOS

> ARNHEM CENTRAL > ARNHEM, THE NETHERLANDS, 1996-

Arnhem Central is a vast complex—totaling 160,000-square-meters—comprised of a transfer hall, offices, shops, tunnel, and underground parking. The project is also the nexus for six different transportation systems. The Arnhem Central started design in 1996 and is being constructed in phases with a projected completion date of 2007. Prior to delving into designing this high-density project, van Berkel and Bos carried out a "deep planning" study. With this planning methodology, they look at all possible sources of information, conditions, networks, issues, etc., to produce the optimum framework for expediting the project.

The main visual attraction of the Arnhem Central is the Terminal Hall that rises, bends, and folds onto itself to create an event space that is experienced by almost everyone who traverses this complex. To generate this digitally feasible form, van Berkel and Bos used the analogy of the "Klein bottle" diagram to conceptually integrate the multiple conditions that fold through the public space, generating one singular form for the Terminal Hall.

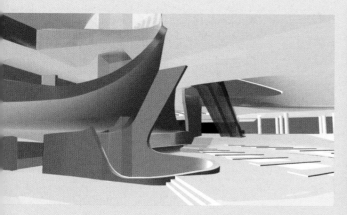

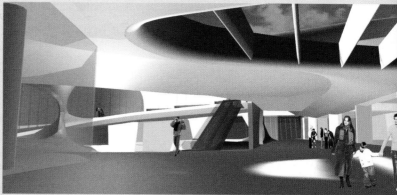

UN Studio's winning invitational competition entry for the new Mercedes-Benz Museum is a simple, smooth building envelope that visually spirals upward, gently wrapping a double helix structure with a trefoil plan and a triangulated atrium/void space. This highly complex and stimulating interior volume is comprised of six double-height and six single-height exhibition spaces that are situated around the atrium/void and are attached by gently sloping ramps. By stacking the program for the museum, van Berkel and Bos were able to create a landscaped plaza that is both raised and leveled and integrated with other Mercedes facilities such as the test course and future development. This new building's sinuous exterior metallic form—which is visible from the hills and the highways—also becomes a metaphor for movement, performance, and scalelessness as cars speed past.

XEFIROTARCH

HERNÁN DÍAZ ALONSO

> THE GRAND EGYPTIAN MUSEUM > CAIRO, EGYPT, 2002-

Hernan Diaz Alonso's entry for the Egyptian Museum Competition is an unassuming undulating form that straddles the arid landscape of Egypt. On closer inspection, the horizontal, asymmetrically disposed structure is very complex. The low-lying augmented formation is the result of juxtaposing programmatic needs with circulatory paths. The Grand Egyptian Museum's sinuous building form is figuratively grounded in the cultural history and very reminiscent of viewing a Michael Heizer sculpture—only a few will ever experience the projected condition from an airplane, or a computer screen.

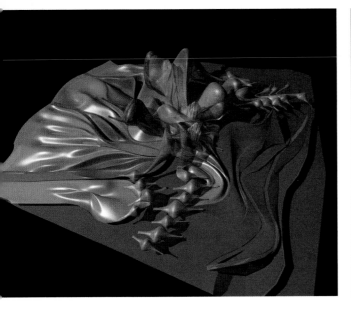
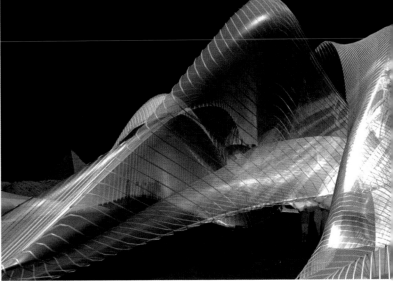

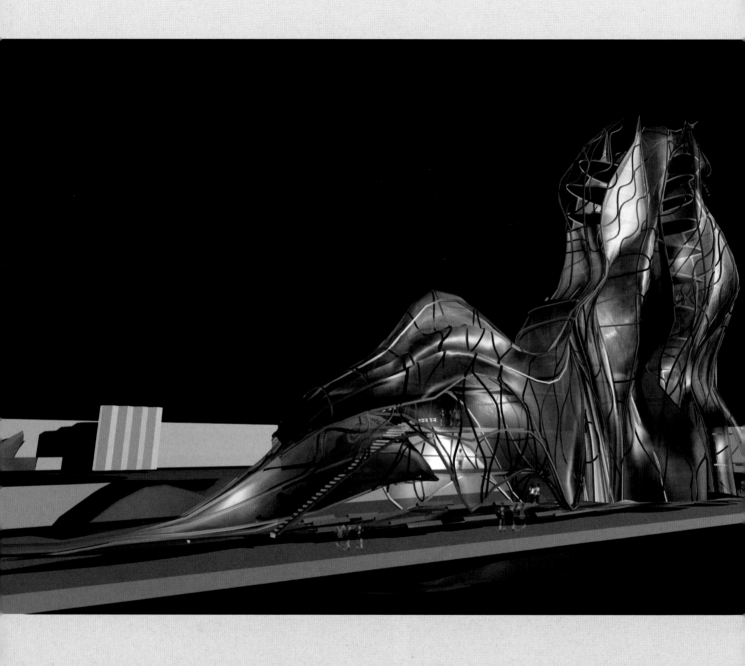

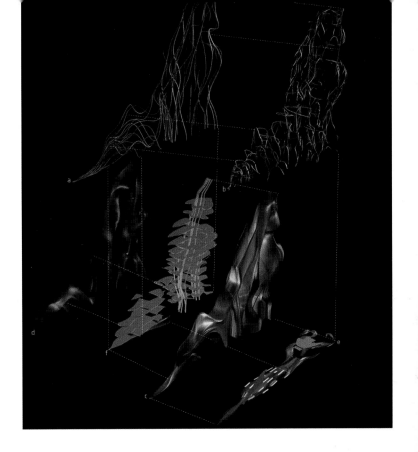

The U2 Tower competition proposal by Hernan Diaz Alonso signifies the trajectory that architecture can achieve when digital literacy and fluid thinking merge. This vertically, horizontally, and diagonally disposed multi-use tower solution also blurs defined programming. The top of U2 Tower's canted prow is a recording studio, while the lobby—situated at the ground floor—is porous to the city and acts like an enclosed "public square." The U2 Tower's intricate structural system is filled with mostly live/work spaces that vary in configuration to reflect the realities of heterogeneous social interaction; this is reflected in the organism-like form.

Diaz Alonso refers to the building's character as "Arach" (Gaelic for dragon), emphasizing the anthropomorphic metaphor of this highly sculptural and structurally complex form, rendering it almost humanlike and all-knowing. The metaphorical and figurative aesthetics generated ideologically illustrate the advancement of twentieth-century modern architectural discourse beyond the predigital, abstract normative character of architecture.

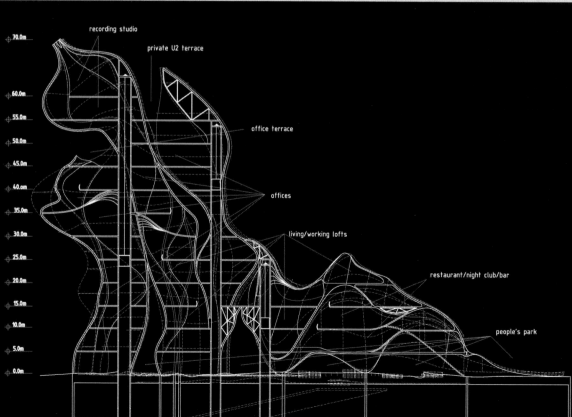

recording studio

private U2 terrace

70.0m

60.0m

55.0m

office terrace

50.0m

45.0m

40.0m

offices

35.0m

30.0m

living/working lofts

25.0m

20.0m

restaurant/night club/bar

15.0m

10.0m

5.0m

people's park

0.0m

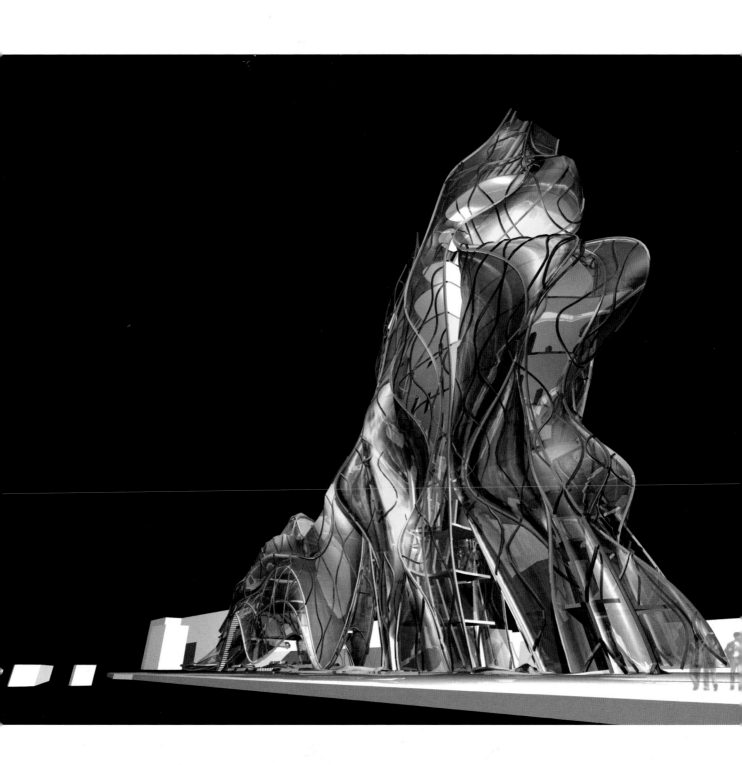

INDEX

CONTACT INFORMATION

ARCHI-TECTONICS > www.archi-tectonics.com

ASYMPTOTE > www.asymptote.com

PRESTON SCOTT COHEN > www.thomaserben.com

dECOi > www.decoi.org

NEIL M. DENARI > www.nmda-inc.com

THOM FAULDERS > www.beigedesign.com

FIELD OPERATIONS > www.fieldoperations.net

FOREIGN OFFICE ARCHITECTS > www.f-o-a.net

DOUGLAS GAROFALO > www.garofalo.a-node.net

IWAMOTOSCOTT > www.iwamotoscott.com

JAKOB + MACFARLANE > www.jakobmacfarlane.com

JONES, PARTNERS > www.jonespartners.com

KOLATAN/MACDONALD > www.kolatanmacdonaldstudio.com

TOM LEADER STUDIO > www.tomleader.com

GREG LYNN/FORM > www.glform.com

MARTIN + BAXI > www.martinbaxi.com

WILLIAM MASSIE > www.massiearchitecture.com

JüRGEN MAYER H. > www.jmayerh.de

NOX > www.noxarch.nl

OCEAN D > www.oceand.com

PATTERNS > www.p-a-t-t-e-r-n-s.net

REISER + UMEMOTO > www.reiser-umemoto.com

ROY > www.roydesign.com

JOEL SANDERS > www.joelsandersarchitect.com

SERVO > www.s-e-r-v-o-.com

SHoP > www.shoparc.com

STAMBERG AFERIAT > www.stambergaferiat.com

SYSTEMSARCHITECTS > www.systemsarchitects.net

UNSTUDIO > www.unstudio.com

XEFIROTARCH > www.xefirotarch.com

PHOTO CREDITS

Kevin Dwarka: 2-3, 76, 79

Archipress 4-5, 28(20), 29 (21-22)

Benny Chan: 6-7, 68-73

F. S. Lincoln Collection, Fred L. Pattee Library, The Pennsylvania State
University Libraries: 14(1), 16(2), 17(5)

R. Buckminster Fuller Estate: 16(3,4)

Huntington Library, San Marino, California: 17(6)

Collection of Whitney Museum of American Art, New York, New York: 18(7)

Archigram Archives/Dennis Crompton: 21(10)

Julius Shulman: 23(12)

Jan Staller: 32(29)

Valerie Bennett: 90-91

Timothy Hursley: 24(13), 33(32)

Peter Mauss/Esto: 35(35)

Paul Warchol:42-43

Christian Richters: 50-55,227

James Haig Streeter: 92, 94

Satoru Mishima: 93, 95, 96-97

Henry Urbach Architecture: 21(11)

Nicolla Borel 110, 111, 113, 114-5

Eileen Costa 207(right)

David Joseph: 207(left), 208

Keith Mallie: 209

ACKNOWLEDGEMENTS

It is a rare moment when you have the opportunity to revisit an earlier published essay, expand and retool the argument to be inclusive of a broader ideology as well as thank the individuals that have assisted in bringing it to fruition twice. This book *Next Generation Architecture* is an expansion of an earlier, 48 page exhibition catalogue *Folds, Blobs + Boxes: Architecture in the Digital Era* shown from February 3 to May 27, 2001; at The Heinz Architectural Center at the Carnegie Museum of Art in Pittsburgh, Pennsylvania.

Numerous individuals have assisted in bringing *Next Generation Architecture* to fruition. First and foremost is Richard Armstrong, The Henry J. Heinz II Director at the Carnegie for his unfailing support that allowed the earlier exhibition and related publication to become a reality as well as his gracious support of this expanded publication and Drue Heinz whose generous patronage established the Heinz Architectural Center.

Words cannot express my gratitude to the architects and their staffs whose work is featured in this book. They generously shared their time with me, discussing projects and related methodologies. I also want to thank my friends and colleagues who shared their knowledge, helping me establish the framework for predigital and digital architecture: Aaron Betsky, Ned Cramer, Jeffrey Kipnis, Reed Kroloff, Madeline Grynsztejn, Tracy Myers, Philip Nobel, Joan Ockman, and Terence Riley. A special note of thanks goes to Mark Robbins for his insightful foreword.

I especially wish to thank David Morton, senior Architecture editor, and Steve Case, editor, for their friendship and persistence to expand this short essay into a substantial publication; designers Sara Stemen and Dung Ngo for creating a book that reflects the ideology (with a special note of thanks to Dung for bringing this project to closure). Finally, I extend my utmost appreciation and affection to my wife, Louise, and our son Hugo, for their unconditional support.

Joseph Rosa

San Francisco, 2003